EMPOWERED
BY DISCOMFORT

ALSO BY CRISTINA M. RAMIREZ

A Gift To Our Readers

Download the FREE companion workbook
to Empowered by Discomfort.
In it you will find templates for the suggested
exercises, as well as other goodies to help you
through your journey.

www.EmpoweredbyDiscomfort.com/workbook

Or, scan here with
your phone!

TESTIMONIALS

"I found Cristina's coaching program at a time when I was very unhappy with my life and myself. Through working with her I began to see the beliefs that were limiting me, keeping me small and making me feel trapped in my own life, and I found the power to change them. I learned to work through my fear of failure and instead embrace the discomfort of new experiences as a chance to grow. I have become a much more empowered and confident person with a vision for myself and my family that I know I have the skills and courage to achieve."
—*Katie, Michigan*

"Cristina has helped me to find the inner strength that I never knew I possessed. I am now brave enough to really stand up for myself for the first time in my life and to make the positive changes that I have dreamed about for so very long. I am happier and more at peace with myself. To put it simply, Cristina is a gift."
—*Erica, Vermont*

"I am not the same person I was when I first encountered Cristina. The training changed my life radically with a confident mindset and opened my eyes to all the healing and growth opportunities in front of me. Your mindset training changed me and continues to have a ripple effect on all my people."
—*Alison, Illinois*

TESTIMONIALS

"I can see the difference. I got my confidence back. I'm like, okay, there you are!"
—*Mayra, Texas*

"I think the major difference that I've noticed in me, and I'm sure people around me, have noticed too, is believing in myself, actually having more faith thinking, I can do it. Before I wasn't so sure."
—*Taryna, Kansas*

"Because of Cristina, I learned that I'm a lot stronger and more capable than I ever believed I was. I thrived in my business, gained the confidence to start a 2nd one, and boldly stepped out to tackle other roles I would have avoided before. This example has made a huge impact on my children and all of the other children I've had the privilege to coach or teach."
—*Staci, Iowa*

"A lot of things have changed for me — the person that I was before vs. now is completely different — I'm a very confident & happy person now!"
—*Isabel, Kentucky*

"If it wasn't for Cristina's guidance and support I would not be where I am today. What she has done for me has been a true blessing and I am so grateful to have been coached by her."
—*Claudette, Pennsylvania*

TESTIMONIALS

"Working with Cristina gave me the confidence to step out of my comfort zone and pursue a path that I love. I use the things she taught me about growth mindset every day as a mom, a coach and as an individual and have been so blessed to watch those lessons ripple out to help and encourage others in my life."
—*Cora, Colorado*

"Because Cristina chose to take a chance on me, I now have the confidence to be true to who I am and advocate for myself as a mom and a businesswoman!"
—*Teana, Washington*

"Cristina has pushed me outside of my comfort zones and has given me the self confidence that I can build a powerful & impactful business as a mom."
—*Sheila, Florida*

"It is almost surreal because it seems like a dream at first ...I'll get there when ... and then all of a sudden it all comes together. It really does!"
—*Jessica, Florida*

"Because of Cristina I was able to help a 5th grader gain the self-confidence to make friends. This is just one of my many kiddos I've been able to help thrive."
—*Kristi, California*

CRISTINA M. RAMIREZ

EMPOWERED
BY DISCOMFORT

DashStrøm
Santa Fe, New Mexico

CONTENTS

THE END OF THE WORLD AS I KNEW IT - 13

1. NO PRESSURE, NO DIAMOND:
THE 20% POWER PRINCIPLE OF DISCOMFORT - 25

How Daunting Decisions Led to the Discovery of Power - 26
Doubting the Power Principle - 40
How to Identify Your Discomfort - 49
Allowing Others to Feel Their Own Discomfort - 61

2. THE FIVE SUPERPOWERS FOR CHANGING YOUR LIFE - 67

3. THE POWER OF THOUGHTS:
YOU ARE WHAT YOU THINK YOU ARE - 77

Why Life is a Risky Business - 85
Own It to Get Over It - 90
Things Don't Happen for a Reason - 96
Zoom Out and Chill Out - 99

4. THE POWER OF WORDS:
WORDS BECOME SELF-FULFILLING PROPHECIES - 107

Awareness is the Root of All Change - 111
Seven Phrases to Change Your Life - 116
Five Words That Define You - 124

CONTENTS (...)

**5. THE POWER OF BELIEFS:
STORIES YOU ACCEPT AS TRUTH - 131**

The Real Truth About Beliefs - 133
Nothing is Impossible - 138
How to Uplevel Your Belief System to Support Your Growth -143
How to Compare Without Despair - 155

**6. THE POWER OF ACTION:
NOTHING CHANGES IF YOU DO NOTHING TO CHANGE IT - 163**

Change Starts with Giving Yourself Permission to Change - 164
Gratitude is the Goat - 173
Make Amends to Find True Freedom - 179

**7. THE POWER OF RESULTS:
2+2 MUST EQUAL FOUR - 189**

Results Breed Confidence -194
Don't Confuse Results with Goals - 199

8. THE NEW BEGINNING - 205

ABOUT THE AUTHOR

ACKNOWLEDGMENTS

To Diego & Felipe - My Everything

To Nana, Papa, Carina, Stacey and Rita
Thank you for sharing Joe with me

In Memory of
Joseph Ramirez
October 9, 1964 - December 9, 2021

*Our wedding picture in the courtyard where we met
at St. Jude's Church in Miami, Florida.*

IT'S THE END OF THE WORLD AS I KNOW IT

AND I'M NOT FINE

IT WAS the Monday after Thanksgiving in 2021 that all Hell broke loose. Joe, my husband, was going into surgery to remove a cancerous tumor from his kidney. He had been diagnosed 7 weeks prior. The night before, he ordered a steak for dinner at our hotel in Albuquerque…The one where I checked in as a wife, but checked out as a widow.

I brought the steak up to the room as he was too weak to sit at the restaurant downstairs. At $37 I was pissed he only took two bites. *Typical Joe,* I thought. He was gregarious and a larger-than-life kind of guy. The type of guy who tipped well regardless of the level of service, who gave $20 bills to random buskers on street corners, who was the first person my boys would ask for something as they knew he'd say yes. I decided to keep my mouth shut. He could barely hold the fork, much less eat a ribeye, and that broke my heart. Here was the man I loved with whom I created our family and life for almost nineteen years, reduced to skin and bones. I looked at the almost intact steak and held back my tears. I could barely recognize the man in front of me. Instead, I smiled, helped him to the bed, and asked how he was feeling.

"By tomorrow at this time I will either be recovering, or I'll be dead," he said.

Little did he know there was a third option: living nightmare. If you just looked at him, you'd know he was a very sick man. He was so thin you could see his bones through the fleece he wore, his eyes had sunken into this face, and his skin tone had gone from olive to yellow. My husband, who skied four times a week in winter and hiked daily during the other three seasons, could barely walk. His back was hunched down, as if to hold his stomach in place, bent over by the pain. He was constantly nauseated and overall miserable.

What we didn't know at the time of his surgery, was that his cancer had traveled from his kidney to his heart forming a clot. That clot was going to cause a heart attack at any moment. It could've happened at the Thanksgiving dinner table where he struggled to smile for a family picture. It could've happened when we stopped at our favorite spot on the Rio Grande on the three-hour drive from our home in Taos to Albuquerque, or in the elevator of the hotel.

Instead, his heart finally stopped beating in the Operating Room—which, all things considered, was a better place than any of the alternatives. Joe ended the day intubated and in the Intensive Care Unit. He was only alive because machines would do for him what his organs were now incapable of doing on their own. One forced his heart to beat, another his kidneys to filter his blood, and the ventilator would breathe for him.

He was in and out of consciousness, and for the next ten days I felt I was in the twilight zone: not alive, not dead, but not able to fully understand what was happening. I was in fight mode, stressed beyond belief, and focused on doing more than feeling. There were only two emotions I could access: love and fear. Every day I came to see him as soon as visitor hours allowed me to and navigated the million questions, consents, decisions, and procedures doctors required to keep him alive. By day eleven, Joe had had enough. We knew each other so well, we could speak without words, which comes in handy when you are intubated with a ventilator. So, I understood when he mouthed "Help me" through his breathing tube. But I didn't know how. I grabbed my journal and wrote out the letters of the alphabet. We went letter by letter, and if I hit the letter he wanted, then he'd blink.

L - E - T

"Okay, 'let,' I got it. Let you what?"

M-E

"Let me what?" We went to D. And I was afraid of what was going to come next.

He blinked next at the letter I...LET ME DIE.

My heart dropped.

Knowing it's your last day on earth must feel weird no matter how much fentanyl is in your IV drip. I asked Joe if he was scared, and he signaled no. I asked him if he was sad, and he nodded yes. I was crushed. It was absolute powerlessness. He was a stoic, and we spent countless hours talking about

15

philosophy. I knew his sadness was not regret. We lived life on our terms and did so rather unconventionally. In fact, many of our friends thought we were crazy when we announced we were moving to New Mexico for no apparent good reason. No, he was sad because the party would go on, and he would not. He wouldn't see our boys graduate from high school, meet our grandchildren, listen to music still not written. He ran out of time to experience all the things we took for granted we would experience together. This was the start of my journey with the 20% Power Principle of Discomfort.

Joe's death on December 9, 2021, brought with it a tidal wave of grief, helplessness, and hopelessness; a hole so big I thought it would swallow me. It's a gut-wrenching feeling of utter and complete devastation that comes when your husband dies, when your teenage sons become fatherless, when you look around and realize that everything's changed. Our marriage was over, everything we had dreamt of, all that we were working on, and the life we had built together, our family... It all changed at a definitive and fundamental level. There was no going back, and there was nothing I could do but accept it.

I was in despair, I cried in agony wanting for things to be different, my brain couldn't process what was happening as I held Joe's hand and he took his last breath. And even in that deep, horrible moment, I remembered this was not the first time I had thought my life was over.

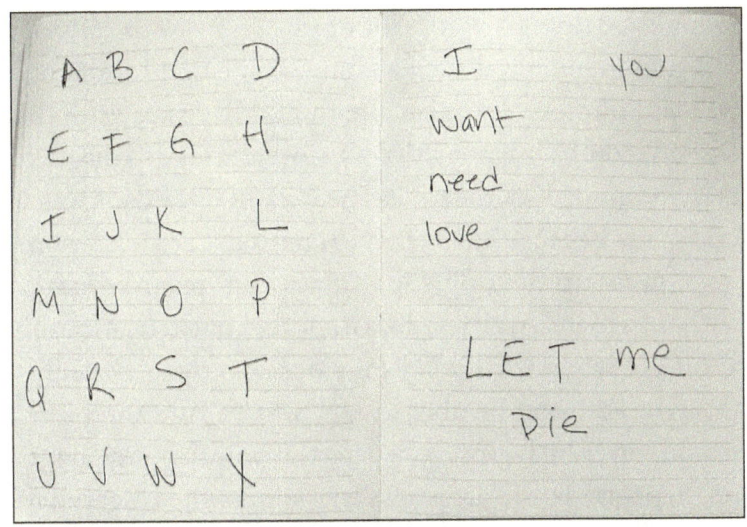

The notebook I held up to Joe so he could tell me what he wanted, and his message to me.

I DEBATED if to share this next story with you. It's about the darkest moment of my life and less than flattering to reveal. In addition to working with individuals and children, I train corporate professionals and was worried it might affect my company's ability to provide our workforce development services. Ultimately, I am not the person I was back then. If sharing this helps even one person, then I am glad I put it out there. You may see me as a successful author and creator of empowerment curriculums. My clients hire me to lead them to their truth and happiness, my students look up to me as their teacher as do my sons. But it wasn't always like that.

It was January 2003, and by the cracks on the gray leather couch, I could see this was the kind of place where

I would be doing a whole lot of sitting. I was thirty years old, and in my mind such a failure at life that I thought it was all pointless. I was on a path of self-destruction that started months—if not years—before and landed me there: at Windmoor Healthcare in Clearwater, Florida. I was in crisis care because I had tried to commit suicide...again.

I grew up hearing, "A woman can never be happy without a man." And here I was, another failed relationship at an age when my biological clock was ticking loudly. I thought I'd never be able to "get a man," and therefore I would never be happy, so what's the point? In my fogged-up, depressed self, happiness was something reserved for the pretty ones, the thin ones, the smart ones. Anyone, actually. Just not me.

I know now that I didn't really want to die. I just wanted to stop feeling the way I was feeling, and I didn't know how to fix that. So, I would continuously hurt myself. Back then, even low self-esteem was a high bar I aimed to reach.

But everything changed one night.

I was in the locked ward, the kind of place where if you wanted to smoke a cigarette (which I did a lot of) you had to use a burner on the wall. That burner had a metal grate around it with a hole; it was big enough for your cigarette yet too small to stick your finger in it.

I knew I belonged there. I would've been the patient who stick her finger to get burned. So, it was no surprise to me, that when I found a razor left behind in the bathroom of my room, I used it inappropriately. But because I was an attention-seeking, love searching, rather pathetic woman at the time, when I was done, I showed the nurse what I did to myself. And that's when the shit hit the fan because you can't have razors lying around in the bathroom of a psych ward.

They put all of us patients in the center of the ward where the gray leather couches were. There were about twenty of us from what I vaguely remember. And there we sat. Waiting. In the meantime, the staff was on high alert and performed in-depth searches of all the rooms. No one was allowed to move from the couch.

All I could focus on was the couple. They had met a few days prior at Windmoor and were in love. Against medical advice, they were trying to escape and get married somewhere. Their families were trying to stop them. They walked around in their pajamas and disheveled hair, holding hands and gazing at each other. It didn't matter this all happened in a *psych ward*, and it certainly didn't matter they were doing the trazodone shuffle from all the drugs they were on. All I saw was a love I didn't have, a stark reminder of the happiness I thought I'd never find. And as I gazed at the drugged-out couple in a real-life Romeo and Juliet scene, I was startled when this man touched my shoulder and interrupted my self-deprecating narrative.

I don't remember his name, but I remember *him* vividly. He had a metal brace around his forehead. It was screwed onto his skull so that it would prevent his spine from moving. It looked more like a torture device than anything else, making it very difficult to look at him without cringing. He was there trying to get sober. His injury came from diving into a pool while drunk: an empty pool. Something he failed to recognize. Hence the broken neck.

He looked at me and said: "Are you happy now? Everyone is paying attention to you."

Here was this Frankenstein's creature of a man, who dove into an empty pool, with freaking screws coming out of his skull, looking down on me with disdain. He was missing his TV show because we were all stuck looking at each other on those gray leather couches.

He. Was looking down. On *me.*

That was my bottom.

It was when reality hit like a cold slap in the face. Me? I was educated in the best schools this country has. I spoke 5 languages. I had been an investment banker and had just started a highly successful nonprofit in Chile. How could he look down on me?

That night I got on my knees and prayed to a God I didn't believe in.

Looking back, it was that night that I started taking responsibility for myself and my life.

Two weeks later, I met Joe at the patio of St. Jude's Catholic Church in Miami, Florida. I needed a light and he was smoking a cigarette, so I went up to him. We were both there for an Alcoholics Anonymous meeting. He had been sober for about six months. It was the day after I got out of rehab. And so, our love story began. From smoky rooms in obscure buildings marked only by a triangle in a circle that indicated that this was where a bunch of alcoholics met to support each other. We got married in May of 2004, at Saint Jude's, just sixteen months after that night at Windmoor. Things could've gone horribly wrong between us. We were barely sober, yet we managed to create an extraordinary family, and a life full of love and adventure.

I am so glad I didn't die in my multiple suicide attempts. I think of what I would never have found, or experienced: Joe, becoming a mom, starting a business, traveling, and all the things that have made me so happy over the past 20 years. I would've missed out on all the love I have felt and was so sure I'd never have. I don't believe a woman needs a man to be happy at all; I just know I eventually got everything I had dreamed of: the family, the house, the dogs, the whole damn thing. I just didn't know I had to get sober to find it. Everything I had the day Joe died came to me only *after* that awful night on the gray couch.

That's why when Joe died, I knew I didn't die with him, even though it sure felt that way. I remember the first time I walked into my house after being with him at the hospital for eleven days. My world came crashing down; it was real. He would never go there again, and yet everywhere I looked there he was. His car keys on the bowl next to the door, his reading glasses he must have forgotten on the side table next to the couch, his favorite coffee mug still sitting in the dishwasher. Photos, books, shoes, sweaters, all of his things were there but he wasn't, nor would he ever be again. I knelt on the floor and cried without consolation; something I would repeat often during the first year. How could this have happened?

But if I sifted through the panic, the trauma, and the shock. If I focused enough on what was deep inside of me instead of the craziness at the surface, I could see there was an inner source of strength that seemed to whisper: *You've thought your life was over before, but the best was yet to come. There will be light again.* I didn't just believe that voice was true, I *knew* that to be true. That didn't mean I would be able to stand up, wipe my tears and get to work on this new life I needed to build, but it gave me hope. It helped me "do life" when all I wanted was to hide under the covers and cry. That knowledge became an unshakeable belief, and I am going to teach you the tools I used to get through the worst year of my life in this book. So that when you face your inevitable challenges, big or small, you too will be able to face those challenges from a place of empowerment. When I give you specific instructions of how to use a tool, you will see this symbol:

I THROW down some tough love here. Not because I am mean, uncaring or don't have empathy for the struggle you may be going through. In fact, I believe that honesty without compassion is a form of cruelty. I have a *lot* of empathy, but I also see through your pain to the possibility on the other side. Self-pity almost killed me in my addiction, I am not willing to stand on the sideline and watch someone sit in their discomfort just because it is the polite thing to do. The stakes are high here. The world needs you. I will teach you to rise up when you feel like hunkering down. I'll tell you the truth of what I know and of what I experienced. Sometimes I wish I was funnier and "lighter," because it might make you more open to what I am going to show you in this book. But that's just not who I am. You may disagree with me or even be upset by what I write, yet I promise that I will also stand in my truth, act with integrity, and show you exactly why and how I think like I do.

I have included lots of stories and anecdotes, mostly from my personal experience. I am no different than you. I have also included stories from clients I have worked with over the years when these will help clarify a topic. All client names have been changed to respect their privacy. You will see my client stories are all from women who wanted to start a children's fitness business. Those are the clients I have worked with most before beginning my more recent coaching practices and workforce development programs.

Still, I encourage you to doubt me, be critical of what you read. If you go through this book with a skeptical mind, and eventually agree with me, then your belief will be infinitely stronger than if you blindly believed me just because I said so. If you doubt and continue to disagree even after you finish reading, then you have affirmed your own beliefs and there is nothing wrong with that. On the contrary, it will lead to more conversation and debate which will make your own beliefs stronger and our knowledgebase a little wider.

Joe & I at one of our happy places in New Mexico.

1.

NO PRESSURE, NO DIAMOND
THE 20% POWER PRINCIPLE
OF DISCOMFORT

BEAUTIFUL THINGS can come from challenges. Therefore, I'd like to introduce to you the 20% Power Principle of Discomfort. I am well aware you might not like, or agree with it. It's uncomfortable after all. And as I mentioned before, I welcome that. In describing it to you, I have tried to keep in mind what objections you might have so that I can address them. For your part, all you need is to approach this with an open mind, be curious as to how this applies to you, and notice any resistance. Triggers and resistance are fantastic indicators that we are talking about something you need to address and heal in your 20% of discomfort.

HOW DAUNTING DECISIONS
LED TO DISCOVERING POWER

IN THE first few days of his ICU stint, Joe was not able to make his own decisions. He was barely conscious, so I was the one they called to give consent. The conversation always followed a pattern. A doctor would come with a piece of paper in his hand. They would explain what was going on, why they needed to do whatever it is they were going to do, and what the risks associated with it are.

"Mrs. Ramirez, when we did the procedure to remove the blood clot from his heart, we realized we couldn't do it vascularly, so we need to do open heart surgery immediately. The risks are blah blah blah and death."

Every day was like that. Every day there was a risk that the love of my life would die. I became numb to the consent requests. I'd listen politely to what they wanted to do and when they started with "The risks are …" I'd roll my eyes and tell them "I know, I know…blah blah blah and death."

The sheer number of life-or-death decisions I had to make in those eleven days was exhausting. But what was even more exhausting was that it wouldn't end once he died.

One of the things that becomes obviously clear immediately after your spouse dies, is that you are suddenly alone. I know, not rocket science. But this loneliness is soul-crushing for all the reasons you would expect. I missed my husband, my best friend, and my accomplice. There was no one to help me make decisions, and there was no one to share the blame if it was the wrong one. You don't realize the benefit of shared responsibilities until there's no one to share it with. In my loneliness, I did the only thing I knew how to do: I turned to self-help books. That is how I navigated so many challenges in the past. But all the books seemed to get me stuck. They would say things like, "It's okay that you're not okay," or "You are now fragile and broken." Indeed, things were not okay, and I did feel fragile and broken, but I refused to make that my story. How could I? Unlike when I was getting sober and recreating my life, I was now a mother with two teenage sons to care and provide for.

My boys were fourteen and sixteen when their dad died. There's never a good time to lose your parents, but we expect it as mature adults. In fact, many of us —myself included— are caretakers for our aging parents. Sometimes their passing, though sad, is anticipated and can bring relief from an extraordinarily difficult period. But losing a parent when you are in high school is not the norm. You are still a child, you still want, need, and long for connection and guidance. Most of your friends still have their parents, so you are thrown into a trajectory that seems different to everyone else's.

The sadness I felt that my boys don't have their dad was often debilitating even though there was nothing I could do to bring Joe back. Yet having children also gave me a north star when making decisions on my own. Any decision I made, from where to have the memorial service to whether we should move houses, was made based on what would be best for my boys. Still, no matter what decision I made, it seemed that someone would be unhappy: I couldn't please everyone, and happiness seemed inaccessible at the time.

WHEN I was in rehab in 2003, after all the stunts I pulled and the harm I caused to myself and to anyone else who loved me, I had to take responsibility for myself. No one could get me sober but me. *I* had to do the deep work, *I* had to have the willingness, *I* had to redefine who *I* was embracing. I became a better, healthier, and saner version of myself. It was a struggle, and it sucked for a while, but on the other side of it was a beautiful life. But that beautiful life and its plans unraveled on December 9, 2021…Now I had to go through that process again. Only this time I was older, wiser, and much more experienced in transformational work from helping hundreds of clients and from my own journey.

I can't tell you how many times I have helped someone through what they believed was a major storm in their life, but which seemed like a drizzle to me. The way I see a client's problem isn't the point. In that moment, it is about how it feels to them. When I tried to minimize what Joe was feeling long before cancer appeared, he would tell me: "Do you know what the difference between minor and major surgery is? Minor is when it's happening to you, major is when it's happening to me." Point taken. I stopped assuming that you and I experience things the same way and stopped judging people when their view of the situation and mine were different. I became more compassionate. And now, I realize at a whole new level that I can't wish away a storm or blow the storm away from someone I am trying to help. All I can do is either give them an umbrella or guide them to a shelter. Perhaps, what I see as difficult, you might find a walk in the park, and ask me why I am making such a big deal out of it; never a good question by the way. The point is, we *all* have our own version of pain. It is up to us whether we turn it into suffering, or to take actions and turn it into something beautiful. I am going to teach you how to do the latter.

One day, alone and crying in my kitchen because I couldn't decide what to make for dinner, I felt the weight of the world on my shoulders. My life had been turned upside down. It dawned on me: I couldn't fix this. Joe was dead. Period. And no matter how much I wanted to fix the pain for my boys, for my in-laws, for anyone who knew or loved Joe, there was nothing I could do. They would have to take ownership of their own grieving process. Although the weight of the world wasn't exactly lifted off my shoulders just because of that realization, there was something *empowering* about it. I stopped feeling responsible for what my boys were going through, I stopped trying to protect them from the pain that was inevitable and began focusing on how to best support them in their *own* process.

This is key: *support* them, don't *fix* them. Trying to fix it for them would've been disempowering; it would be me telling them, "I don't believe in you enough to trust that you can overcome this challenge." Supporting them is a dialogue, where they can then choose how to cope based on our conversation. Thinking that I can fix them, or you for that matter, is totally egocentric. It assumes I have some Godlike power that you don't possess. That is just not true. I simply have some tools that you haven't learned yet and when you do, you'll not only be able to tackle your 20% of discomfort, but you will be able to live in peace *even with* your discontent.

From there, I decided: *Everyone has their 20% of discontent, discomfort, sadness, unhappiness, yuckiness...that particular something...* You call it whatever you want. And there is not one damn thing I can do about it. Joe had it when he died, my boys have it, I have it, and you do too.

....

The goal is not to get rid of your discontent. The goal is to grow and be at peace regardless of what is in your 20% of discomfort.

....

LET'S GET on the same page with terminology. According to the Merriam-Webster dictionary, discomfort is a mental or physical *unease* whereas discontent is a *dissatisfaction*. For our purposes here, I am using both interchangeably. I chose discomfort because to me it is more powerful — physical or emotional unease tends to lead to action where dissatisfaction is something you can tolerate and therefore it can linger for a long period of time without doing anything about it.

I know this 20% of discomfort concept might be a tough pill to swallow, but it's actually liberating. To pretend that everything is awesome all the time, like we see on social media, is a lie. Not only is it exhausting to keep the appearance that all is well, but it also actually hurts us. It loops us into a narrative of *I'll be happy when...* because you think there will be a time when you will be 100% content and feel like the Instagram photos you scroll through. That just isn't true. There is no destination, no point in which finally, everything is okay. This is not depressing, this is empowering. To accept that life will inevitably include discomfort is a relief. Then you don't need to freak out every time something goes wrong. It's just part of the deal. And if I accept that premise for myself, then I can accept it is true for others. I don't need to make myself responsible for what is in your 20% of discomfort. What a relief to let go of the belief that I had to fix my kids' grief. They had to own it, just like I had to own my process of getting sober, and now I had to own recreating my life as a widow.

··

Everyone will have their 20% of discomfort.
And it's up to them to fix it.

··

Moving Goalposts

I'll be happy when… Ugh. Have you ever had that thought? I'll be happy when I have more money. I'll be happy when this deadline is met. I'll be happy when my kids go to school and I have more time for myself. If a client says this to me, I know they are in for a rough ride. There is no 'when.' 'When' is a myth, a construct. 'When' is believing there is a destination, a point in time you will get to and there you will finally be free, happy, content, comfortable, and happy. Some people might tell you that only happens when you die, I am here to tell you that is not true either. Sure, there are moments of bliss and fulfillment, but I am a firm believer that you *never* get 'there.' I am also a firm believer this is not a bad thing. When Joe understood that his condition was terminal, he felt like he was still in the middle of the road, and he didn't have time to get 'there.' There is no destination. Instead, life keeps getting bigger and you never get to a point where you are 100% satisfied. It's such a hard topic to understand, so let me illustrate it with a client story.

Mary's Story

Mary is a firecracker: aggressive, diligent, and willing to do the work. I helped her start her first business and her goal was to generate $5,000 a month. Mary would tell me, "Oh my God, Cristina, if only I could make $5,000 a month my life would be so dramatically different. I can't even. Can you imagine? Oh, that would be the best thing ever! I'd feel like I made it. I could afford to do the things I want, oh, it would be magical indeed."

And so, we began working to make that a reality. *Easy-peasy*, I thought, *I do this on the daily for my clients. Let's get Mary to her $5,000 a month and that will be life-changing and 'Oh my God.'* She just can't wait to get there. Mary did the work that needed to be done, and after a few months, her business was up and running making about $4,000 a month.

"Wow. If I can make $4,000 a month, I know I can make $5,000 because I am almost there. But can you imagine if I made $7,000 a month?" And then Mary told me, "Oh my God, Cristina, can you imagine? $7,000 a month? All my problems would be over, and I wouldn't have to worry about anything again. It would be the best thing ever. Can you help me get there? That would be just so incredible! Okay, $7,000. That's the goal."

We continued working together, and Mary's business grew. She was so focused, dedicated, and committed that she continued to jump through hoops and overcome obstacles, and made it to $6,000 a month. "Hey Cristina, how cool would it be to have a business that is six figures? That's $8,800 per month. Can you imagine that? Holy crap that would I.N.C.R.E.D.I.B.L.E. I can't even."

But on the journey there, Mary struggled a bit more. There was something about that six figures that made it harder and the obstacles got bigger: hiring a team, marketing, taxes, etc. One day, in tears, Mary lamented to me, "Why-oh-why am I such a failure? Why can't I ever find peace, why is it always a struggle, what am I doing wrong?"

Meanwhile, Mary completely forgot her initial goal was $5,000, she was now consistently making $7,000. It was not that she was a failure or that she struggled more than most. She was actually successful! But Mary kept redefining success. The goal posts keep moving. You never get 'there.' It's like the end of the rainbow you think you see, but when you get there, it has moved further away. It's elusive. But while you are making your way toward the changing goalposts, you are hitting the goals that you set for yourself, blowing past them without recognizing it, and making your life and goals bigger.

So, in regard to the 20% of discomfort, it will always

be 20%. Getting to $5,000 a month didn't solve Mary's discomfort or discontent because she was now focused on $7,000. She was not suddenly just 10% discontent. Thinking bigger and redefining what was possible served to make her want more, and that's a wonderful thing. So, her percentage of discomfort didn't get smaller, her container got bigger.

"Wait, Cristina, are you telling me you never get to feel good about yourself?"

WE'LL TALK about this again later, but that is the crux of the whole thing. You should celebrate every achievement big or small along the way. You will have many reasons to feel good about yourself, while also feeling empowered to grow even more. Anytime you move the ball forward, even if just a tiny bit, it's enough to celebrate. Stop for a second, pat yourself on the back and tell yourself, "Good job!" You just moved the ball forward. *That* is where the magic is way more real than telling yourself, "I'll be happy when…" Knowing and accepting you will always have 20% of discomfort, and validating every step big or small as you address that discomfort, is the game changer. Facing your 20% of discomfort from a place of empowerment and peace… That is the secret to a healthy, happy, and fulfilling life.

Why 20%?

Before we get technical here, 20% is not a *technical* number. It's just a number I believe represents most of us. Unlike Pareto's law which states that 20% of your actions give you 80% of your results, there is no science backing my 20% Power Principle. So, don't get stuck there. If you feel better using a different number, knock yourself out. The principle is the same: there will be a part of you that is content and a smaller part that is discontent. Always.

....

Lean into the discontent. Don't hide from it. That is where your opportunity for growth lies.

....

HERE'S AN example: Let's say your discomfort comes from not having enough money to go on vacation this year. That sucks. I get it. But you really want to take your family on a trip, so you pick up some extra hours at work, and save up enough to take them on a small vacation after all.

You solved problem A: having enough money to take your family on vacation. But it's not that you are now only 10% discontent because you figured it out. You are still 20% discontent because your container is bigger.

Yep. So now the source of your discontent is no longer that you don't have money to take your family on a vacation. You dealt with that. But maybe on vacation you realize just how much your work is sucking the life out of you. And that becomes your 20% discomfort. This, in turn, leads you to have a conversation with your boss and he re-assigns some of your tasks.

Once you have new and interesting tasks, you realize you could do your boss' job better than he does. Now that becomes your 20% of discomfort until you prove yourself and get a promotion. Again, the 20% never goes away — your life gets bigger. Whereas before you were worried about not being able to take your family on vacation, now your discomfort comes from not being properly valued at your job.

It's a never-ending cycle. As it should be.

KNOWING THAT everyone has 20% of discomfort at all points in their lives, and that allowing them to work through it is empowering them to grow their container is liberating. I didn't have to fix anyone, and if I make a decision with the best of intentions and it turns out to be wrong, then it is wrong. I can apologize and make amends where I can, but if you still don't like it, well, then that is part of your 20% discomfort and you have to handle it. I make the best decisions I can with the information I have at the time. You can handle your response to that decision. I'm not trying to be cold or uncaring, but it's not all that bad. Now you have something that you are discontent with, and that will cause you to take an action and grow from it. That's why I called it a *Power* Principle, because it gives us the courage to change.

Therefore, there are two parts to this. First, you should understand your discomfort is inevitable, but will not crush you. On the contrary, it empowers you. When you reframe discomfort as a flashing sign that says, "Go here to grow," you stop being afraid of feeling discontent. You stop trying to make it go away by numbing it, procrastinating or hiding. You welcome the discomfort because you know there will growth on the other side of it. It may even be beautiful. Second, when you let others handle their own 20% of discomfort, you are giving them a gift. You are telling them, "I believe in you enough that I don't have to fix it for you. I know that when you do, you will have grown and feel empowered for having done so."

This concept of letting others go through their discomfort without feeling the need to fix it for them, was inspired by the serenity prayer. I don't consider myself religious, but getting sober, I went to an Alcoholics Anonymous meeting every day, including the one where I met Joe. And every meeting I have ever been to, regardless of where in the world I was, started the same way: with the Serenity Prayer. And at twenty years sober and counting, I have been to a lot of them.

God, Grant me the serenity to accept the things I cannot change,
The courage to change the things I can,
And the wisdom to know the difference.

I was taught to view it like this:

*Accept the things I cannot change…*I can't change you or anyone else. I can't change anything outside of myself.

*Courage to change the things I can…*I can only change me, so the courage to change me.

*The wisdom to know the difference…*Well, that became easy to understand, not so easy to practice.

I CAN'T change you. I can't change my kids. I can't change that Joe died. I can only change my attitude towards those things over which I have no control. If you are committed to your view of the world and not open to debate, there's little I can do about it. And here's the clincher: I don't have to. That's your belief that you own.

Let's say that your belief is that all people from a certain neighborhood are crooks. I happen to be from that neighborhood, and I own a super-adorable gift shop smack dab in the middle of it.

Your belief affects me because you may not shop at my store, or you may tell people that this neighborhood is full of crooks, and they should never go there. If they believe you, those people won't be shopping at my store either. So that kind of sucks for me and that is part of my 20% of discomfort. I may not have the best location for my store. But I own it, and I can say the Hell with you and look for people who don't think that way about my neighborhood and invite them to my store. I cannot change your mind if your mind is set. I can talk to you, debate with you, show you how I'm actually a nice person, but if you don't *want* to change, there's nothing I can change about you. Letting you sit there with your ideas, even though I think they are misaligned, is power.

I understand it is very difficult to allow someone to think they are right when every cell in your body believes they are wrong. I struggled with this as my political views are the opposite of my parents' and we often argued about them. But in the end, they didn't want to see my point of view. And truth is, I wasn't open to theirs either. Until either of us was willing to stop defending our position and actually listen with the intent to understand, nothing was going to change. And letting go of the need to have them think like me, or even understand me, was both freeing and empowering. It allowed us to have a meaningful relationship where we each agreed to disagree and be done with it.

DOUBTING THE 20% POWER PRINCIPLE

I KNOW saying "It's good to feel bad," might be counterintuitive, or perhaps you disagree with me. As I mentioned before, not only is it okay for you to doubt me, but I encourage it. So, let's go through some objections you might have so far.

What if I am more than 20% discontent?
What if I feel like my discomfort is 40% or 80% of my life?

I TOTALLY understand the feeling of being overwhelmed and that things may feel like they suck way more than just 20%. Sometimes it might *feel* bigger, as if the majority of your life was in turmoil. If you remember my stint in rehab, I was suicidal, and I thought joy and happiness would never come to me. Suicidal thoughts surely are more than 20% of discontent, aren't they? I felt worthless, and I focused on that feeling almost to the exclusion of anything else. But I wasn't worthless. I know that now. Therefore, it might feel like you are mostly unhappy, but what if you were to make an inventory of your life? Could it be that you are not noticing the largeness of it and not seeing everything you have going for you? In my case, I realized I needed another lens, and I believe you can discover a new lens, too.

Remember Mary who was not seeing all she had

accomplished on her way to her six-figure business? Trust me, when Joe died, I felt like my world came crashing down and I might have punched you in the face if you told me that what I was feeling was just 20% of discomfort. At that moment, I couldn't hear it. In time and using tools I will teach you in this book, I could see that it was indeed true. As much as it hurt, and as much as I loved my husband, there was more to my life.

Isn't this another version of Toxic Positivity?

TOXIC POSITIVITY is a catch-all term but in general, it is when you deny the 'bad' times or the struggles that we inevitably face in favor of forced and unyielding optimism. When things go wrong, you don't allow yourself —or someone else— to feel the emotions and the disappointment in favor of quickly turning it into a lesson or a positive. Using phrases like "Look at the bright side," or "Everything happens for a reason" with someone who is in the midst of a trauma or struggle might make them feel like their emotions are being invalidated.

That is not how I operate though. I'm not saying you don't have problems. On the contrary, we *all* have problems; it's the fundamental piece of the 20% Power Principle of Discomfort. I am not invalidating your feelings; I understand that it feels that way. I also understand that at times, things are harder than at other times. My first year as a widow was the worst year of my life, by far. I could've technically said I was 95% unhappy.

But even during that year, I used the tools that I am going to teach you here to get myself to understand that even in my darkest moment, there was light. This was a crappy situation my boys and I were going through, but the grief was a small section of the entirety of my existence, and the extraordinary pain forced me to pay attention and change. I'm not saying that you must recognize the benefit of a hard situation immediately, but can you see that on the other side of it might be light?

So, while I don't question your feelings, feelings aren't facts. Your challenge can become your biggest strength. If you can't suspend judgment this hot minute, and you are huffing and puffing underneath your breath, that's your 20% of discomfort which I can't do anything about. You own it.

Ouch.

And just like I am letting you own this, you will learn five superpowers that will allow you to empower not just yourself but your children, co-workers, friends, partners—anyone really—so they don't stay stuck in a disempowering story and victims of circumstances, but instead build resilience.

Resilience is not toxic positivity. Resilience doesn't mean that uncomfortable things, or heck, even crappy things, won't happen. But building resilience will allow you to confront your discomfort and grow your container.

The point here is, I'm not invalidating your discomfort. I am teaching you that you can have discomfort and live a wonderful, empowered, peaceful and happy life.

Why are you boxing everyone into the same category of 20% discomfort?

GOOD POINT. I agree, we are all different and come with a different set of experiences and beliefs we inherit as they are passed down from generation to generation. But again, I have a belief that we are all more alike than we are different. When you cut yourself, or when I cut myself, we both bleed red. And when it comes to belief systems, I've encountered many.

I grew up Catholic. My parents actually met at Saint Patrick's Cathedral in New York City. Eventually, they moved to São Paulo, Brazil, where I was raised and where they took my sisters and I to church every Sunday. When I was fifteen, we moved to Casablanca, Morocco, a Muslim country, where five times a day the *adahan* (call to prayer) was broadcast from the mosques. At seventeen, I was sent to an all-girls boarding school in Connecticut to complete my senior year. My high school years were spread in three different continents —South America, Africa and North America— and speaking a different language in each: Portuguese, French/Arabic and English. Believe me when I tell you that I understand a thing or two about diversity. And maybe, because I do, I can tell you that when we strip down all the cultural capes that we identify with, we tend to be more alike than different.

My Muslim peers love their children as much as I do, my African American friends do too. Weird huh? My South American friends are always searching for ways to be better humans, just as my European friends. Amazeballs. We might do things differently, but our human needs are universal. We all need to feel safe, loved and that we matter, regardless of who we are. So, when I generalize the 20% Power Principle I do it with 100% certainty that it applies to pretty much everyone. Show me one person who doesn't have that discontent or discomfort, and I will show you someone who is hiding from their own truth. I don't care who you are, where you live, what color your skin is, or who you pray to.

Don't complicate things. The only thing I really, *really*, need you to understand about the 20% Power Principle is that you and I, and everyone else has a certain amount of discomfort in our lives. And we should not be afraid of that, we should embrace it because discontent is what points us in the direction of where we need to change if we want to grow.

I am only 20% discontent in certain areas of my life.
In other areas I am less and others more.

AND YOU'D be just like most of us. Think of it as 20% in general. If you experience no discomfort with a certain aspect of your life, there really is no need to act in that area. Our discomfort level is relative to our desire for growth. For example: When I'm snowboarding with my kids, I am afraid of falling and hurting myself. I am in my fifties, and when I fall it hurts and it takes me longer to recover than when I was in my twenties. I am perfectly content riding on easier trails and not doing anything crazy. My sons, on the other hand, compete in the United States of America Snowboard and Freeski Association (USASA) Snowboarding Series and try to make it to the National Championships every year. They are not nearly as afraid as I am to hurt themselves; partly because they are young (and stupid, as teenage boys often are), but mostly because they want to get better. And if they want to get better, they will need to learn new tricks, and before they master those tricks there will be a whole lot of falling going on.

Their desire to perform a new trick on the snowboard, makes them discontent that they don't know how to do it, yet. And because they can't perform those yet, they might lose a competition or not qualify for Nationals. It's that discomfort, that fear of not making it, that pushes them beyond their comfort zones to try new things. They *know* that learning a new trick will hurt, but their discomfort with not landing it will keep them going until they finally get it. Since I don't have that particular discontent, I am not even going to try. It's the discomfort that motivates you.

The other thing that happens is I can be totally content with my current snowboarding ability and not want to change it. Great, no problem. But I can be discontent with another aspect of my life, for example, health or finances or relationships.

If I am struggling with my child, for example, that would probably occupy a lot of my 20% until I mend or accept that situation. But meanwhile, there might have been something going on with my finances that I wasn't paying attention to because I was so consumed by the issue with my child. So now that I have freed up some of my worry bandwidth

—*pop!*— out comes the issue with my finances, and that becomes what I pay attention to in my 20%.

The 20% Power Principle doesn't tell you that you have to be 20% discontent in every area of your life. It is there to hold space for that discomfort, in whatever area of your life it shows up, and to call your attention so that you change and grow.

What if my 20% is coming from something that can't be changed?

As YOU will see when we talk about the beliefs necessary to embrace this Principle, one of them is that nothing is impossible. And we talk about that in Chapter 5. So, the first thing is to be sure that your discomfort really can't be eradicated.

Now, even someone like me who wholeheartedly believes nothing is impossible, cannot go against the laws of nature. You can't be born and adult and die a child. Also, there are tragedies and suffering that I must accept. I am with you; I hear and empathize with you. But you must grieve for what was and is no longer possible, let that grief be inside your 20% of discomfort and then grow your container.

When Joe died, if you would've told me that this discontent was an opportunity for me to grow, I would've told you in a very matter of fact way to f*** off, *not* because what you were saying wasn't true, but because I wasn't ready to hear it, yet. The pain I felt was like nothing I had ever faced, and it felt like I was 90% miserable.

It was from that space that I understood the 20% Power Principle at a deeper level. It felt like losing Joe was 90% miserable, but it wasn't. I just wasn't able to zoom out yet. Therefore, if you are still grieving a loss: of a life, of your health, or anything that cannot be changed, you need to allow yourself to grieve. But know that once you are past the pain, your container will be bigger and you will be able to see how this tragedy, this difficulty, this unfairness can and will lead you to become someone different. It will create a bigger container.

"Acceptance is the answer to all of my problems." This is one of the quotes from the *Big Book* of Alcoholics Anonymous which still stays with me. The quote continues: "When I am disturbed, it is because I find some person, place, thing, or situation—some fact of my life —unacceptable to me, and I can find no serenity until I accept that person, place, thing, or situation as being exactly the way it is supposed to be at this moment."

....

Until you accept the reality, the same reality you don't want to accept because it is not what you expected, or wanted, or believed, you will not have peace.

....

AND ONLY when you have peace will you understand that you have grown your container so much that this thing which you cannot change becomes a smaller and smaller part of your life.

I know this is hard, it is hard for me to say it, too. When I first began to feel this way, I felt I was cheating on Joe's memory and felt guilty about that. But it's not that the love I have for Joe is smaller or that I am forgetting him. It goes back to the same point that made him sad on the day he died. Life was going to go on, and he wasn't going to be a part of it. No matter how hard this moment is, it will pass. How you feel today is not an indication of how you will feel tomorrow, and that is what gave me hope when the grief was at its worst. Life will go on, and this moment will not lose its importance or relevance to you...But it will be a smaller part of your life which gets bigger with every breath you take.

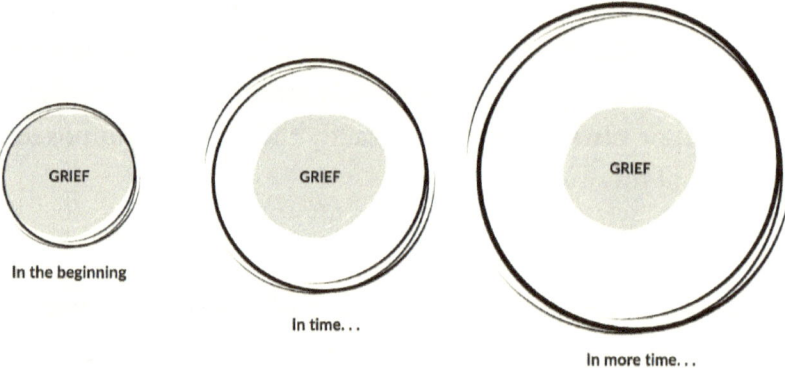

In the beginning

In time. . .

In more time. . .

HOW TO IDENTIFY YOUR DISCOMFORT

ONCE YOU know what is in your 20% of discomfort, you can then use the five superpowers I will teach you in this book to grow your container. When we talk about things we know, we can classify them into three buckets:

1. You know what you know (I know how to speak French).
2. You know what you don't know (I don't know how to speak German).
But oftentimes, we live in number 3...
3. You don't even know what you don't know. You have a general feeling of discomfort, but if I asked you, "*What's wrong, exactly?*" you may not be able to tell me.

I MIGHT have stirred all kinds of things for you, because when you challenge someone's beliefs head on, you tend to get resistance. And as the receiver, you get triggered. Sometimes triggers are obvious, and you get outraged. Other times they are sneakier, and you need to pay attention to catch them before they spiral out of control. I'm going to go against the grain here and tell you that *triggers are amazing!* They are clarifying events. I'll explain in a moment, but you might be wondering, *Is the 20% discomfort the same thing as a trigger?* Well, they are related. It's as if they were cousins. Not the same person but definitely in the same family.

Trigger is a loaded word. I can tell you what it means to me because acknowledging them for what they are — *clues*— will be one of the most powerful things you can do for yourself. Triggers show you what is in your 20% of discomfort that you need to work on. It's why I call them clarifying events or feedback. And working on those triggers will ultimately help you gain control over things that might seem out of control right now.

But most of us, when triggered, become angered and feel the need to defend ourselves. What if instead, we took a breath, and with curiosity took a look at what's underneath? What if we reframed triggers as feedback? As if there were flashing lights and arrows pointing you in the direction of what you need to pay attention to. So much easier said than done, but ultimately, such a life-changing tool.

One of my biggest triggers is *the feeling of powerlessness.* So, for me, it's *not* a coincidence that I have focused on empowering others. This comes from a history of being the youngest in a family of five and feeling like I had no choice and no voice. It was never up to me where to go out to dinner or what movie to watch. And though it might not have been intentional, the way I experienced my childhood was as one where I didn't matter: I was different, and I was teased mercilessly. My older sisters were the fun ones, the popular ones. I was the nerd and stayed home alone on weekend nights while everyone else went out to party. This caused all kinds of issues for me. I believe this feeling of powerlessness was one of the biggest contributors to my many addictions. If I felt cornered, ridiculed, or that someone was imposing their power over me, I would become enraged. I'm not exaggerating here. I lived with an uncontrolled rage against power of any sort. And hence, when Rage Against the Machine became popular, I would yell out the lyrics of "Killing in the Name Of" as if it were my anthem.

I have resolved all of this with my family, so the root cause of my trigger is no longer there. My parents both passed away in 2017, and I had a great relationship with them. I am very close to my sisters and love them dearly. But when I feel like one of the "powers that be" is crushing my ability to do something, just because they can, then that childlike feeling of powerlessness and rage comes roaring back. It has the power to take over and wreak havoc unless I deliberately interrupt the pattern and reinterpret that trigger.

Yet, the core of that trigger – powerlessness – is still there. Today, it is mostly reflected in large companies who exert power over my life. In fact, Joe & I had a code word for my trigger: COMCAST.

I WAS nine months pregnant, and Comcast scheduled to arrive at my home between 9:00 a.m. and 12:00 p.m. to fix the cable. This was before the streaming era and since we lived in a building wired by Comcast, it was either work with them or stick to the four open television channels. *Okay*, I thought. *I'll take the day off, wait for them in the morning and run errands in the afternoon.*

At 11:45 a.m., there was still no sign of the cable guy, so I called customer service, waited the obligatory million hours to speak to someone, who then asked all the questions to verify my identity only to tell me:

"I'm sorry Mrs. Ramirez. They are running late, but they should be at your home between twelve and two."

This same process was repeated at 1:45 and 3:00pm. Each time I was told they were "almost there." Until my final call at 4:45PM where I learned that after taking the day off, spending it in my 2x4 apartment, bored out of my mind without tv, bleary-eyed from reading all day, pregnant and about to pop a baby out, hot, uncomfortable, and generally miserable…Comcast wasn't coming. Not only where they not coming, but they held me hostage all day.

I was livid. And triggered: *Who do they think they are that they can have me sit here all day waiting for them?* I called customer service again.

"I'm so sorry Mrs. Ramirez, I can credit your account with $25 for this inconvenience."

$25. That was what eight hours of my day was worth to them.

I was so upset that I did the only thing I can do when I feel completely powerless and frustrated and triggered: I cried. I *ugly* cried because I completely lost control of myself and my emotions. But when your trigger is *powerlessness*…I felt stuck, backed into a corner. There was nothing I could do. No matter how many times I called, pleaded, explained, and lashed out, I just kept making things worse.

When you are triggered, nothing productive will happen. The emotions are so heightened and so overpowering that they cloud your ability to think rationally. Of course, it was not the end of the world that Comcast didn't come, but it *felt* as if my entire existence was worth $25.

*There is nothing you can't make worse
by reacting to a trigger.*

WHEN TRIGGERED, it is best to just let it flow through you. And I strongly suggest putting yourself in time out. When you are agitated, you will probably lash out at anyone who tries to help you. When in a deep emotional state, you only want to hear that someone agrees with you and validates the anger you are feeling.

So just spare yourself —and them— and take some breaths, go for a walk, jump up and down, whatever, just calm the heck down. There is nothing that you can't make worst by acting while being triggered. And here is some more bad news, if you try to push it down or fight it with some rational personal development tool, it will come back out with more power the next time you are triggered. But eventually the emotion will pass, much like a wave. If you fought against it, like I did with Comcast, you can look back and see the path of destruction left in its wake. It will make you feel awful because that is not who you probably want to be, but you felt that it was out of your control.

Whatever the emotion is: anger, rage, sadness, fear, even grief…it passes. Then, and only then, can you handle your 20% of discomfort. In the midst of the storm that 20% will not feel like power. Instead, it will feel crushing and something you must absolutely destroy because it is so damn uncomfortable. But once it finishes, then there is a lull. That is where you can reflect on what that trigger was and what you can do about it next time.

Just like a child. If a two-year-old is throwing herself on the floor, screaming and crying about how she wants her candy, trying to appease her will do nothing. She just has to go through the disappointment so she can eventually learn to regulate her emotions. We adults throw grown-up tantrums and oftentimes find it difficult to regulate our emotions. Introspection comes only once you are calm.

Then you can ask yourself, "What was it about this situation that triggered me so much?" Notice I didn't say, "Why am I still so triggered by this stupid stuff when I know better?" Introspection only works if you are neutral. There is no shame or blame and much less judgement. It's just where you are in your journey, that is all. Don't give your trigger even more power by berating yourself for falling into the spiral yet again. Be kind and acknowledge that you are now asking questions about it so you can be a better version of you. In time and with practice, you will begin to recognize and catch your triggers much sooner so that you don't have to spiral all the way down in order to get the memo that this is something to pay attention to.

But you need to pay attention and stay aware. There is a lot that goes on in our brains that we are not even aware of. We can't be! We are bombarded by thousands of stimuli every second, and it is impossible to pay attention to them all. As you read this, think about everything your brain is processing, from your bodily functions, your heart, breathing, the temperature outside, the color of the page of this book, to the sounds around you. There's just too much to focus on at once.

THERE IS an experiment known as the Invisible Gorilla. It is from the research by Daniel Simons and Christopher Chabris, and you can see it on YouTube. In the video, three people wearing white t-shirts pass a basketball to each other. Then there are three people wearing black t-shirts and they too pass a basketball to each other. You are asked to count how many times the people in white t-shirts pass the ball to each other and you are shown the video for about 30 seconds. At the end, the experiment asks you how many times the people with white shirts passed the ball, and you are given the answer. You are going to think you were pretty smart for getting it right. But then, you are asked:

"Did you see the gorilla?"

It is revealed that in the midst of all the ball throwing, a person dressed in a gorilla costume walked across the room, stood in the middle of the players, waved at the camera and you didn't even notice him. You were so focused on counting the passes that you missed an entire gorilla! You were selective with your attention. So bizarro. But it is a powerful example of focus. Just because you focus on one thing, doesn't mean there aren't a bajillion other things going on.

So, unless you make an effort to go back and examine your triggers, you will be held hostage by them. You will not pay attention to them, just like the gorilla. Make the effort. It will be well worth it.

Once you recognize, "Wow, I was really angry back there," just ask yourself what about that situation touched a nerve. Be curious. Explore it. Journal about it. Just stop for a moment and think about it. Soon, you will begin to see patterns and be able to identify the situations that trigger your emotions. And then when those situations arise again, you will be able to process your emotions better.

Powerlessness... Just yesterday there was a charge on my credit card from a free trial that I signed up for and didn't cancel. $340. I called the company and there was no customer support to talk to. I was on hold for over 30 minutes before I gave up. The unconscious me was throwing a tantrum because I have so many things to do other than figuring this out, but I know this type of situation is still a trigger to me. I hung up and called my bank to see if I could dispute the charge. I'm not saying that I wasn't annoyed, or that it didn't suck, but instead of being at a ten and throwing an adult tantrum I stayed at a five and didn't behave like an idiot.

Therefore, next time you are inpatient waiting at a red light, you lash out at your partner, yell at your kids, or become uncomfortable enough to pout, throw the tantrum you usually throw. Get it out of your system, feel the feelings, roll with the wave. But when it passes, consciously take the opportunity to recognize, "Holy cannoli...I am triggered. This is my chance to explore my 20% of discomfort." Eventually, when you become more aware of your triggers and your discomfort, you will be able to catch the wave of wrath earlier on; just like I did with my credit card charge. That is a ninja power, because then you can interrupt your trigger pattern at any point instead of riding it all the way to the bottom. Think of it as an elevator. You can get off at any floor. You don't have to wait to get to the basement. Interrupting your trigger only works when it first starts rumbling, but the world will thank you for stopping it.

THE LIFE INVENTORY

You don't have to wait to be triggered to figure out what is in your 20% of discomfort. Another tool you can use is the Life Inventory. When I coach clients, it's the first thing we do. I ask them to look at different areas of their lives. These are:

Finances
Work & Career
Health & Fitness
Relationships
Recreation & Free Time
Personal Development
Community & Contribution

Write this list for yourself and rank your level of satisfaction in each area from one to ten, where one is *not satisfied at all* and ten is *totally satisfied.*

You'd think this is a no-brainer, but it's not. I have done this exercise countless times. In fact, I do it at the beginning of every quarter to see where I am at. It helps me choose if and how I want to be intentional about working in a specific area of my life. What I find interesting is that things shift and change over time. And there is a temptation to measure your satisfaction based on what other people expect, or even to what other people believe is satisfying. So, it's *very* important to be true to yourself. I'll give you an example:

I DID this exercise midway through my first year as a widow. If you were someone who didn't know me, on the outside you might look at my life and think, "*She really ranks low on the relationship scale. She's a hermit, doesn't have a romantic partner, and barely goes out with friends.*" While all that was true, none of it bothered me. I ranked myself very satisfied in my relationship space because the relationships I cared about were solid. I was perfectly satisfied. Perhaps, in the future, I might want to be more social or develop other relationships and if that desire hits me, then I'd probably rank lower in relationships because it is not where I am. But at the time, and even now, I am perfectly satisfied not just with my relationships but my definition and intention in that area of my life.

Go ahead and take a deep look, be extremely honest with yourself and write down your level of satisfaction in each area *before* reading the questions that will come next.

Now THAT you completed your Life Inventory, you probably have some areas that score lower than others. Those areas are your Opportunity Areas. It's what's active in your 20% of discomfort right now. If it weren't, you wouldn't have scored it low. Let that sink in for a second, and now let's examine it.

- Is your Life Inventory fairly balanced with some areas where you rank high and a couple where you could work on?

- Does your inventory reflect your priorities? Are your numbers higher in the areas that you have prioritized and have been deliberately focusing on? Were you intentional in those areas?

And probably *the* most important question:

- Is there an area of your life you'd like to change? And if so, are you *willing* to do the work to change it?

WILLINGNESS IS essential. In the example above, pretend your belief is that you have always been a little unhealthy with your eating habits, but so have your parents and they live good lives. Then, this is not an area you are motivated to work on because you are not willing to change it. No judgment. That is okay, as long as you are okay. However, if that is just a story you tell yourself so that you can look in the mirror and be content but deep down you want better health, then that's in your 20% discomfort and you can tackle it. No one can make that decision for you, and no one will really know, so take this opportunity to be super honest with yourself. Now that you have your inventory, you have a base.

You can't improve upon what you don't measure.

NEXT, WRITE a list of all the things that are part of your discomfort *and* that you are willing to change: you are motivated to do something about it, but perhaps you don't know how. Be specific, don't write "Everything." That's not helpful. If you are struggling with your health and you want to change that, then write "I would like to take better care of my health." You don't need to know *how* to do it, just that you realize the discomfort, and that you are *willing* to do something about it.

Got it?

Great. Keep that area of discomfort in mind as we move forward. For our purposes and to continue on our journey together, you should have two things by now.

1. You have come to a place where you can accept the premise that you are 20% discontent—not 50, not 80, *just 20*.
2. You know what is in your 20% of discomfort right now that you are willing to change.

If that bothers you, or you are triggered, *stop reading*.

Journal about it, be gentle with yourself and take the opportunity to explore why you feel this way. Reframe the trigger as feedback to guide you as you move forward. What is it about this premise that is making you uncomfortable? That is a tremendous start in dealing with your current 20% of discomfort.

If you are good to go, let's talk about recognizing and letting go of the 20% discomfort someone else might have, even if you are desperate to fix it.

ALLOWING OTHERS TO FEEL THEIR OWN 20% OF DISCOMFORT

ONE OF the biggest gifts you can give *anyone* is allowing them to handle their discontent. It's hard to see someone struggle, I know that. It's especially hard if we care about them whether they are a friend, partner, child, co-worker, employee... anyone. But it's that struggle that will form their character and build resilience for the next struggle and the next and so on. Allowing someone to feel sadness, emptiness or stronger, darker feelings is painful. It might even feel as if it hurts us more than it hurts them. I say this with a caveat that if someone has an emotional disorder, is depressed, or similar they should be supported by a trained professional.

Recently, I was walking the dogs with my older son. It was a particularly hard day for me. I was stuck in fear and definitely not being an example of how to handle my 20% of discomfort. It happens sometimes, and it's important for our children to see our struggles so that they are normalized, and it shows them that having bad days is just a part of life. But when you have them, you can then do something to change them. It shows them resilience and gives them confidence that they will be able to overcome their discomfort as well. Therefore, the first part of empowering others is allowing them to see the real you in your discomfort and give them a role model to mimic when they inevitably face theirs.

On this walk, my son said, "Dad would always tell me he had a bunch of stories to share with me but that I had to grow up a little bit before he could share them with me. Sometimes I wonder what those are."

My heart broke into a million pieces. Again. There was sadness in his voice, a longing for his dad, and an awareness that those stories died with Joe. It's not something I can fill for him; I didn't even know what those stories were.

Grief is cruel.

Often, us parents believe we know what is best for our children. And most times we do! We have the benefit of experience, of seeing the bigger picture that a child or a teenager just doesn't have. But instead of making the decisions for them, it is important to teach them to make those decisions for themselves. Provide support, give them perspective if needed, but let them sort it out knowing you are just a call away if they need help.

It helps me to remember that when major things have happened to my kids, I was right there but nothing I could've done would've prevented it from happening. Felipe fell off his bunk bed when he was four and required 12 stitches. Diego broke both his tibia and his fibula playing catch with a friend. Their dad died. Our cat died. They broke up with girlfriends. All these left physical and emotional scars I couldn't fix for them.

Here's a story of how to allow a someone to own their 20% discomfort. This story is about my son but it's the same concept for a friend, partner, employee, parent. In a nutshell: just hold space.

WE TRAVELED over five hundred miles to Arizona for a weekend snowboard race. It's a discipline called boardercross—just imagine motocross, but downhill, on snow, and riding a snowboard. It is scary. This competition was organized in heats where the morning races determine the seeding for the afternoon final race. That's the one, and *only* one, that counts. Felipe, who was twelve years old at the time, had done well all morning. If he kept it up, he was sure to get on the podium. This mattered a whole lot to qualify for Nationals. Consequently, there was a lot riding on this two-minute race. Felipe started strong. Not only was he in second place, but he was closing the gap to first place.

And then he fell.

I saw it happen. It was a small wobble, but while on the ground getting up, the two other competitors who were behind passed him leaving Felipe in fourth (and last) place. I saw him place his hands on his head as if saying "Noooo—" The chance of Nationals was passing by him, just as his competitors had.

Now, Felipe is generally stoic. He doesn't enjoy wearing his feelings on his sleeves. But a mama bear knows when her cub is hurt. All sorts of good advice crossed my mind about how to console my child who was doing his best to keep it together. The athletic coach in me was thinking that I should tell him how he still has two races to qualify for Nationals, how the course was hard, how this is only his second winter, how he will learn from the experience, and how he could analyze what he could do differently next time. The mom in me wanted to ask for a "re-do" so my baby could do better. Or a way to get him a prize of some sort or buy him a giant sundae because everything is better with chocolate. The mindset coach in me, however, knew just what to do: *hold space.*

Hold space so he can feel the disappointment.
Hold space so he can feel the pain.
Hold space so he can slap his hand on his head and say, "Oh no, no, no."
Hold space for him to feel all the feels.

AND HOLDING space is hard to do, especially when it comes to your child. But holding space is exactly what you should do for anyone who is processing a difficult emotion from grief over the loss of a loved one to the loss of a snowboard race.

It is hard for us to see someone we love in pain. We want to fix things, and we want them to feel better as soon as possible because they're not feeling good makes us highly uncomfortable.

....

We want to fix them because of how their emotions make us feel.

....

BUT DENYING them the space to feel the hurt and the pain is what really hurts them in the long run. They will try to move through discomfort as fast as possible by shoving the feeling deep down, somewhere hidden in the subconscious mind. But it *will* come out, at some point, and chances are that it will surface in an inappropriate way, maybe by eating or drinking too much, or by giving up in competition. Not holding space for them to feel the hurt will hurt our children more.

I can already hear you. "Do you mean to tell me that one loss of a snowboard race is going to create a future alcoholic?" Of course not. But the habit of stuffing down the little disappointments in life, not feeling the feelings, and trying to gloss over them will create big problems down the road. So, hold space. Let them go through it and they will come out the other side. You don't have to fix someone who is struggling just so that you can feel better. All you need to do is hold space. What does that mean? Here's what I did:

I told Felipe I understood how disappointed he was, and how I wished I could take it away, but I couldn't. I told him to feel everything he needs to feel, that he was safe, and that I would be right there for him as soon as he wanted or needed to talk about it. Then I took my book out and began to read, while he sat in front of me with his head buried in his hands. Every once in a while, I offered him water or food, both of which he declined with a shake of his head. We were there for about an hour. I was biting my tongue, I told myself, "Hold space, hold space, hold space, and let him go through it so it can come out of him." But boy was that hard!

Eventually, his snowboarding goggles that he had been hiding behind, came off. He looked up, asked for something to drink, and when it was time to watch the awards ceremony, he was still upset, but he was composed. He composed *himself*. I didn't have anything to do with it.

Later that night, before heading to sleep, I asked if he

was feeling better. That's when we were able to talk about what went wrong, what he could do about it now, and in the future. Only then did my "Learn from Your Mistakes" sermon come out. I waited until the time when he would be able to listen, when he was not lost in the emotion of a massive disappointment.

Let's say your spouse didn't get the promotion he thought he was a shoo-in for. That would be a disappointment, for sure. You can tell him how much you love him and how you think he is amazing regardless of his job title. You can be available when he wants to talk about it, you can listen, be extra kind and do something special for him, but it's not your responsibility to make him feel worthy. Give them space to work through it. Lots and lots of space. **It's simple, while not necessarily easy. But it is fundamental.**

2.

THE FIVE SUPERPOWERS FOR CHANGING YOUR LIFE

Now comes the fun part where we get to meddle in your discomfort and work through it! In order to do that, I am going to show you a sequence of mindset concepts and then give you tools to help you tackle each one of them. I call each of the parts of this sequence a superpower because each holds the potential for lifechanging results. The other awesome thing about it is that you already have these, all you need to do is recognize and develop them.

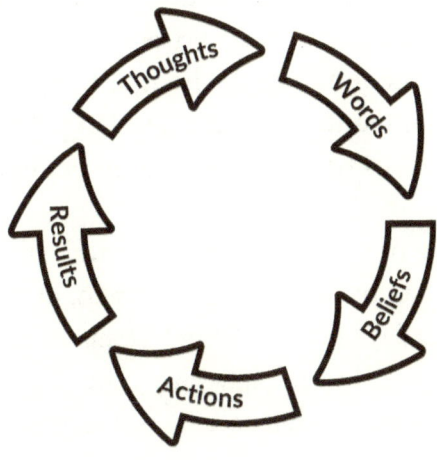

I STUDIED Philosophy at Wellesley College. I loved metaphysics and my favorite philosopher was Descartes. What I loved about him was that he challenged the beliefs of his time. He attacked the idea that our senses provide us with accurate information, deconstructed his existence and reconstructed it only with things he could be certain of. He explained there is a difference between the mind and matter. For example, have you ever had a dream that was so realistic that when you woke up you had to really think and be sure it wasn't real? How do you know that your dream is not your reality, and your reality is not your dream? Or if you ever did a guided meditation that took you to a forest, you can feel the damp ground or hear the birds in your mind. How do you know you really weren't temporarily transported? *Poof.* Mind blown. There is a whole world that happens between your ears and there is something or someone who does the thinking. Awake or asleep, someone has to be behind the thoughts and that someone is you. You are the source of thoughts and, as Descartes famously formulated, *cogito ergo sum:* "I think therefore I am." Thought is the basic building block of who we are. It is what allows us to have an identity; since there is the presence of thought there must be the presence of someone doing the thinking. The power of thought is the start of everything else in our lives.

I TAUGHT one of my empowerment curricula to middle schoolers. It's a challenging age to teach, but I got them interested from day one. Here's how: I empathized with their sense that they really don't have any control over anything. Someone tells them what to eat, allows them to buy or not buy a game, what time to sleep, and what school to go to. They have to go along with the plan because they are usually too young to emancipate from their parents. They have a voice. They can tell the parents what they want. They can challenge us with their behaviors, but they really don't have control. Except for one thing: what goes on between their ears.

I told them: "It drives parents bananas, but we cannot force you to think something unless you want to do it. We try to influence you, sometimes we force you to do something and sometimes we even bribe you! But what you *actually think* is the one thing we cannot control. You have the power. That is your superpower."

We and therefore our thoughts, are influenced by our environment, the media we consume, and the people we hang out with. Later, we will examine the beliefs that were instilled in us by our cultural conditioning. But when push comes to shove, no one can force you to have a thought.

You should have seen how their eyes opened wide. Because it is true of middle schoolers, adults, and every other human. No one can make you think something without your permission. And whatever you think, is your reality. Your thoughts control everything. If you think you can do something, you can. If you think you are smart, then you are! If you think you are stupid, well, you will behave stupidly. You will look for —and therefore find— evidence for whatever you are thinking. This is called 'confirmation bias.' The world is a dangerous place? You will find evidence of that in the daily news. The world is a beautiful natural wonder to explore, you will find evidence of that too. You look to confirm whatever it is that you are thinking. It's the core of everything. We will dive deeper into thoughts in just a second. But look at this sequence:

Thoughts – Words – Beliefs – Actions – Results

YOU HAVE your thoughts, and you express them out loud through words. Those thoughts and words create stories that, when you repeat them enough and decide they are true, form your beliefs. Beliefs are the gatekeepers. They are what will allow you to act or prevent you from acting. And the actions you take, or do not take, determine your results. When you reflect on these results, the cycle begins again. Let's see some basic examples to drive the point home:

Thoughts: There was a hard math problem in my test, and I figured it out. I must be smart.
Words: "I am smart."
Beliefs: *Because I am smart, I can do things that others can't.*
Action: I am going to sign up for all AP classes
Results: I graduate high school with a bunch of college credits.
Thoughts: I should be a freshman, but I already have the coursework for sophomores.
Words: "I am smart."
Beliefs: *...and on, and on.*

One more:

Thoughts: *I forgot to bring brownies to the office party, I am overwhelmed.*
Words: "I'm such a space cadet, I can't believe I forgot them at home."
Beliefs: *I am overwhelmed and can't think of every detail for everyone.*
Action: Argue with my kids for not picking up their room, which is a mess, because I haven't hounded them to do it because I don't have time to do everything I need to do.
Results: I say mean words to the kids which makes me feel horrible.
Thoughts: *I'm a terrible parent because I am overwhelmed.*

It's all connected and understanding your superpowers is the basis of being empowered because you can change at any point. You can change your thoughts, your words, your beliefs, or your actions, and it will change your results. Your new results will then inform a change in your thoughts and words, and these will support you in still more new thoughts, which will create a new basis of belief that will direct your actions, and which will give you more of those results and on and on it goes.

I think I am beating a dead horse here.

Emotions

I WISH it were a simple linear sequence, but unfortunately, it's not. We have emotions to contend with. For our purposes, let's define an emotion as a feeling-response to a thought. Our emotional responses give our thoughts particular meanings, and at the same time, the meanings we give to thoughts provides them with an emotional content. For example, let's say you are walking down the street and you see a penny on the ground. If you don't attach any particular meaning to noticing the penny, you will not have an emotional response. But, if your grandmother was your role model, and every time she found a penny, she would carefully polish it and put it in a special place, and you miss her terribly, the fact that there is a penny lying on the ground stays the same, but now it's entangled with a meaning or a memory and produces and emotional response. Perhaps you smile thinking of grandma, or perhaps you cry because you miss her.

Emotions are fuel to your beliefs, usually they act as a strong affirmation of why your beliefs are true. They bring intensity and that can be both a good or bad thing depending on the belief that it is intensifying. Let's work with an example to really drive this point home: I found a perfect calm place by the river to write on my journal. I get settled, take out my water bottle, and as I begin to write I hear a noise coming from the brush.

> *Thoughts: There is someone out there, I don't know who it is, why would someone be in the brush?*
> *Emotion:* Fear.
> *Thought: What if it is a serial killer?*
> *Emotion:* Even more fear.

WHEN IT comes to our sequence it would look like this:

> *Thoughts: There is someone out there and I don't know who it is.*
> *Words*: "Anyone there?"
> *Emotion*: Fear.
> *Belief*: (already present, now reinforced) *The world is a dangerous place.* This belief is confirmed by the presence of the footsteps and my fear.
> *Action*: I don't like taking chances, so I get up and move spots.
> *Results*: I have less time to write on my journal and feel frustrated because my plans were interrupted.

IF, HOWEVER, my belief is that the world is full of wonder, the emotional response to my thought would be different and lead me to a different action.

THAT SEQUENCE, then, could be:

> *Thoughts: There is something out there and I don't know who it is.*
> *Words*: "Anyone there?"
> *Emotions*: Wonder/curiosity.
> *Beliefs: The world is a wonderous place. This belief is confirmed by the presence of a noise coming from the brush.*
> *Actions*: I wonder what that is, get up and go check it out.
> *Result*: I spot an elusive red tail fox!
> *Emotion*: Excitement.

EMPOWERMENT IS being aware of your sequence and the effect emotions have on it. Once you master these concepts, you will be able to control your emotions, so they work for you, support you in empowered beliefs from where all things are possible. Unchecked, emotions will keep you stuck in your present belief system and sabotage any attempts you make to change.

Knowing how this sequence and how your superpowers work are key to tackling your 20% discomfort with confidence. Often, we tolerate things because we fear what would happen if we changed them. That is often why people remain in relationships even though they are not happy or stay in a job even though they are not fulfilled. In that mindset, we believe that staying where we are is better than going through the discomfort of changing. However, we turn our 20% discomfort into a Power Principle when we accept that discomfort is part of life, and when we know how to effectively work through it. If we can trace back the beliefs, words or thoughts that lead us to our actions, then we can take control of them, and influence our results. You might think, "Sure, that is easier said than done." I've said the same thing when presented with a new idea. Yet, I hope that understanding this sequence will give you a framework for growth, and you can see that changing your life is possible and it's not rocket science.

....

Each of the steps of this sequence is a superpower you already have. You just need to harness them.

....

WHAT YOU will need is discipline to go through it. And before you tell me that discipline has always been a problem for you (it was for me), I want to tell you this: you are already disciplined. But you are disciplined by the thoughts, words, and beliefs you currently hold. You are loyal to those because you are used to what they give you. You don't have to change everything, just the ones holding you back from diving into your discomfort and growing your life container.

3.

THE POWER OF THOUGHTS

YOU ARE WHO YOU THINK YOU ARE

YOUR FIRST superpower is the potential of your thoughts: the building blocks of everything. If you google "how are thoughts formed," you're likely to go down a rabbit hole for weeks. And while I am absolutely fascinated by this, I'm well aware you may not be, so I am going to keep it as simple as possible. I don't want you to go down that rabbit hole right now.

Thoughts, for our purposes, are the stories we create in our mind and that no one else sees. They are individual and private. They can seem very real, but they don't exist outside of ourselves. No one can really read our thoughts unless we express them in one way or another. Only *you* know and own your thoughts; no one can force you to think one way or another without your permission. Thoughts are the building blocks of who we are. They happen spontaneously or deliberately, and the good news is that we can change them whenever we want, though it's not always easy.

As we just saw, thoughts can provoke emotions. I think of Joe, and it produces an emotion. Sometimes it is sadness, other times it's gratitude, but there are others too: anger, longing, grief, etc. I think of a road trip we took as a family and I feel happiness, or if I think of crossing a finish line of a race, I feel pride. Emotions and thoughts then, are often interconnected so that if you can master your thoughts, it will be a lot easier to master your emotions.

Think of it this way: your brain is bombarded by sensory inputs at the rate of 11 billion per second. These are nonnegotiable in that you cannot sense what your body does not physically have the ability to sense. For example, birds are known to use magnetically sensitive particles in their eyes, beaks, and ears to navigate. Humans don't have those sensors, so we cannot navigate using magnetic waves. We navigate using the sights, sounds, memories, etc. that our physiology allows us to use.

Also, your brain tries to be as efficient as possible. Therefore, anything that it learns it stores so that you don't have to learn it again. You don't tell your arm to move, the brain knows how to do that, so it stores that information and frees up "space" to learn other things. Have you ever driven somewhere you go to all the time and when you arrive you have no idea how you got there because you were in Lalaland thinking of something else? Your brain has already memorized how to get to that location.

Even with this efficiency, your brain cannot pay attention to billions of sensory inputs bombarding you every second.

Therefore, we filter out these sensations and only sense what we focus on. These focused sensations are called perceptions; it's as if you were putting a spotlight onto which sensations you want to pay attention to. If I tell you, put your attention on your feet, you'd focus on the sensations that your feet are feeling and not on so much on the taste in your mouth. Whereas sensations are mandated by our physiology, perceptions are negotiable; you get to choose what to pay attention to. We have that power.

Perceptions, in turn, fuel thoughts. *My feet feel are cold; let me put socks on.* In other words, thoughts take what you perceive in the outside world and merges them with your internal world. Let's break this down:

Sensory Input: I scroll aimlessly through social media.
Perception: I stop to watch a video of a clumsy puppy trying to get up a staircase.
Emotions: I feel warm and fuzzy inside.
Thought: I should get another dog.

ACCORDING TO the Cleveland Clinic we have, on average, 70,000 thoughts a day. *Seventy freaking thousand.* Not only is it impossible to pay attention to all the sensations your body is feeling at any moment, you also cannot pay attention to all of your thoughts. Yet, of those 70,000 thoughts 80 to 90% are repetitive. Meanwhile, the more you think about something, the more your brain is wired for that thought and codes these patterns into memories, skills, and a sense of who we are. Here's an analogy. When we go snowboarding, early in the morning, I take the dogs on a walk through the snow-covered woods. It's a small area that connects where we stay to another road.

One night, we got dumped with almost two feet of snow so that the next morning, when I went for our walk, it was really hard to get through the woods because I had to walk through the powder. I was making the way, having to lift my knees high in order to get through. However, this is a popular area and throughout the day people continuously walked on that first path I made plodding through powder. Each person who walked through the path I started, made it easier for the next one. So that by the time I returned in the afternoon, it was a clear path and easy to get through the woods. The same process happens in our brains. When you learn something new, or when you have a new thought, it is harder and takes more effort, yet our brain looks for ways to make this efficient. Soon, with repetition, that thought becomes hardwired into what we call neural pathways.

Back to the driving example. Let's say you have a new job. The first time you drive there it's still new, so you need to pay attention, follow a map and look for markers. Maybe you try a few different routes to see which one gets you there faster, but once you have a favorite route which gets you there efficiently and consistently, you stop looking for alternatives. By the hundredth time you drive the same route, you no longer pay attention to the map or look for markers. Your brain already knows where to go. The neural pathway is created. It's the same with your thoughts. Once you have a thought that you accept, either positive or negative, it's a lot easier to keep repeating that thought than creating a new one. Fortunately, our brains are amazing, and we can rewire those neural pathways so that you create new thought patterns. It's quite easy to do as children, to them, they are constantly having to lift their knees two feet to get through the powder so there is no "preferred way." After the age of twenty-five it becomes harder, though not impossible, to change these neural pathways.

But if we have at least 6,000 unique thoughts a day, how are we supposed to control them or change them? And how do we recode thoughts that don't serve us? Great questions. If you want to know what those thoughts are, all you have to do is look at your world around you. It reflects your thoughts. I know, I know. You can tell me: "I live in a bad neighborhood and am struggling to pay my bills. I work my butt off, and you are telling me that my life is a reflection of my thoughts, not of outside influences that conspire for or against me? Influences such as governments, economics, society, etc.?" It's tricky, I get it. I have often felt that outside influences were conspiring against me too. Here is a story for you:

IN 2018, I decided to expand the reach of EmpowerFit, the curriculum I wrote teaching character development to children through running. I coached moms to start a business and teach EmpowerFit in their communities, and though we are present in forty states (and counting), like most businesses, it was a struggle at first. It seemed that every time I was about to have a breakthrough, something came from left field to sabotage it. That "something" was usually a kid who got sick or a husband who traveled meaning I didn't have the time to work on my business because I had to take care of the boys. Whatever. It was always *something*.

My repetitive thoughts became a story that I couldn't be a successful entrepreneur until my kids grew up. Because of confirmation bias, I then found evidence to prove that to be true. Of course, there were plenty of days where everything was fine, but I didn't notice those. I only paid attention to the ones where someone needed me, and I wasn't able to push my business forward. I used *words* (hint hint) to describe this to a friend. The story went something like this: "I have the vision of what I want to create, it's right there, and I even have a plan to get there but there are these huge blocks between me and that vision. And those blocks are the responsibilities I have to my family."

I remember it clearly. When those words came out of my mouth, I felt like crap. I love my family more than anything else in this world and they are, and will always be, my first priority. And here I was telling someone they were my block to the vision I had for the business I was passionate about.

Shit.

Fortunately for me, I decided then and there to change that thought. And instead of placing my family between me and my goals, I chose to place them behind me, *pushing me towards my goals*. I know it sounds simplistic, but really that's all it takes.

Nothing outside of me changed, but I changed. And the thought that my family was behind me, supporting me, and the biggest reason *why* I wanted to succeed in my business became my new repetitive thought. You can guess what happened next. I had fewer obstacles, and my business began to move forward. Does that mean my kids didn't get sick or my husband didn't travel? No. I don't believe my thoughts alone can change those things, *but* I didn't see those facts as problems anymore. Just things I had to deal with on my journey; part of my 20% of discomfort. Big whoop. In fact, I noticed more and more the days where I was really able to focus. I paid attention to my family and reminded myself they were *why* I was starting this business. And if my kid got sick, it was motivation because once I had my business up and running, I could take all the time I needed to care for him. That is what I focused on, not the story of "OMG, again? How am I ever going to be able to succeed if every time I need to do something someone gets sick?"

That is power right there.

For me, the thought that my family was now behind me, and pushing me to my goals instead of *between* me and my goals was revolutionary. But this is not fairy tale land. It's not that one day I decided and then, magically, I never had my previous thoughts again. Remember, your brain gets wired for certain patterns and emotions, so I had to repeat my new thoughts over and over. At first, these were conscious actions. My initial conditioned response to my obstacles would pop up, "Grrrr…Why is he going to travel again?" and then I had to tell myself, "Nope, old story. This is exactly why I am pushing through; they are my *why.*"

Changing your thoughts requires deliberate action. This is in part because both science and psychology have affirmed the existence of a negative bias. Whereas confirmation bias is where we look for evidence outside of ourselves that show us that indeed, we were right, negative bias is like a radar searching for what is going to go wrong next. In its simplest form, it is a mechanism from our ancestors who needed to remain safe in a world full of danger. Being alert to danger was a matter of life and death and therefore a lot of energy was spent looking for what could go wrong next. At a higher cognitive level, it is believed that negative stimuli are more complex to process than positive stimuli and therefore we spend more time processing that negative stimuli. Easier said: you learn more from your mistakes than your successes. For example, if you wanted to pass an important licensing exam to further your opportunities, but you didn't, you are more likely to spend time figuring out what went wrong. If you had passed, you would be less likely to go back and figure out which parts you did right.

And finally, scientists have researched that when adults make judgements and decisions, they weigh negative aspects more heavily than positive ones. It goes back to that primal need for safety; we believe that by thinking of everything that could go wrong we can then accept the risk because we have thought it through and are okay with the consequences if things do go wrong. Though it's what we naturally do, it doesn't always serve us and often times holds us back from taking risks to change what makes us discontent. In the process of coaching moms to start their businesses, I cannot tell you how many women I spoke to believed it would change their life in a significant way for the better, were qualified and could've been really successful but never took the leap because they got stuck in this thinking pattern. However, the truth is that life is risk, and therefore I think it's important to take a sidestep here and talk about risk and fear.

WHY LIFE IS A RISKY BUSINESS

WE ALL have an expectation of what life should be like. For me, it was having a family, doing meaningful work, raising amazing men, and growing old with the man I loved. But there just isn't any guarantee. Some of these things will be true, and others aren't. I am not going to grow old with Joe, I am not going to retire in northern coast of Portugal with him as we had planned, and there's not a damn thing I can do about that. Living is a risk. We are all daring risk takers. We just normalize certain risks in order to live.

There is no guarantee that our kids will be happy and fulfilled. But we parent them hoping for the best anyway. Most of us assume that if we walk to the store to buy food, that we will come back home in one piece. But that's just not true. For all we know, we could be hit by a bus on the way there.

CONUNDRUM: WE need to feed our family, but we may die on our way to the store. Therefore, we mitigate risk. We cross at the light, we look both ways to make sure there are no cars coming, we go during the daytime. We make the trip to the store as safe as it could be. Yet we accept the risk because the need to feed our family is greater than the fear of potentially being hit by a bus. And though the risk exists, it is considerably low.

I think about this as my youngest son is learning to drive. There are millions of drivers every day in the streets. In fact, there might be a billion. And yet, the majority of them make it safely to their destination. If I look back at all the stupid things I did when I was a teen, it's a miracle I am alive after all the stunts I pulled. You probably have the same thought too because it seems that youth is synonymous with stupidity. The decision processing part of our brains (our prefrontal cortex) is not developed until our twenties. Even knowing that, we still try to protect our children. It goes back to that negative bias. We love our children, we want them to be as safe as possible, and to do fewer stupid things than we did. We set boundaries and rules when a risk seems too big. And yet, it seems that every year in every town, there is some horrific accident with teens involved. So, even if we set those boundaries, tragedy can happen. While at the same time, we must let our children grow - and in this case drive.

What's weird is that many more of us fear flying than we do driving, yet you are much more likely to die in a car accident than on an airplane. It's the illusion of control and frequency. Because we are the ones driving the car, and we do it so often, we have integrated that risk. But the real truth, is that driving is risking your life.

Or think of the millions of cells in your body, and everything your brain does in order for you to function. All the synapses and signals, all the peptides and neurochemicals. And yet, most of us walk around with beating hearts and without having to consciously think about putting one foot in front of the other to get to where we want to go. So much could go wrong at any moment. But usually, it doesn't. Until it does. Like in Joe's case his cells created a tumor in his kidney.

We are driven by a million forms of fear. It is primal and most definitely a part of your 20% of discomfort. Oftentimes, just feeling fear is enough to stop some of us from meddling in our 20% of discomfort; it becomes too much and we feel we cannot possibly handle it. So, we settle in it, thinking we might as well stay here, in our discomfort, tolerating something because at least we know how that feels and we know we can handle it. We do this *even though* it does not serve us. Fear is is the most disempowering emotion of them all; it either stops us from moving forward or causes us to react impulsively and make a mess out of things.

What is one to do with fear? You can't stop feeling it, remember it's primal. But you don't have to live in it. You don't have to put it front and center and let it control you. Your superpowers can help you through it. To be certain: I'm not saying don't be afraid. I am saying be afraid and tackle your 20% discomfort anyways.

However, if you are still in trauma or feeling PTSD, I want to be clear that this is different. If when you go into fear you lose all control, you are likely having a trauma response where you cannot access your objective thinking because your brain is flooded with stress hormones. If when you go into fear it's just that you are triggered and know that on the other side of it you will be okay, then you have access to your logical brain to work through whatever it was that triggered you.

Let me clarify this for you. As I mentioned, my boys are snowboarders, and love doing tricks on their boards. In

2022, they set a goal to perform a back flip. They didn't just go out on the snow and try it; they would've gotten very hurt. There was a progression. First, they consistently landed the back flip on the trampoline, then on an airbag in the snow, and then on their own. Thankfully, they learned this while away at a camp and I wasn't there to watch.

However, doing a flip, on a snowboard, going down a mountain, is *scary*, especially the first time. And when they were hesitant their coach said something very insightful: There is a difference between fear and doubt. If you are scared, you need to push through it. If you doubt your ability to land the trick, you are not ready yet, and you need to practice more before attempting the backflip on the snow.

....

Fear and doubt.
The work is in distinguishing between the two.

....

I WAS afraid of writing this book, but I didn't doubt my ability to do it. Sure, I could feel insecure or as an imposter, but if I look at things objectively, I know what I am talking about and feel confident in my message. Once I realized this, then I could focus my efforts on overcoming my fears that live in my 20% of discomfort and that has stopped me for years from writing this book.

How DO you know if it is fear or doubt? Doubt is a skill-based insecurity: "I am not sure I can do a back flip safely." Fear is: "Oh wow, what if I don't land it and get hurt?" Doubt is overcome by learning more. In the case of my son's backflip, doubt was overcome by asking the coach for help, going back to the airbag, repeating it over and over again, until they landed every single flip on the airbag. Only then did they move to the snow. In the case of writing this book, doubt was overcome by doing my research, getting a fantastic editor, seeking help from experts, and building a team that can help me where I lack skills. Fear is overcome by knowing you did all you could and accepting the risk inherent in doing it. Because as we saw: life is risk.

Sometimes we confuse this and hide in our fear by telling ourselves, "It's just that I am a perfectionist and so I'm not ready to bring my art, music, thoughts, business, whatever, into the world." Perfectionism pretends to be a positive trait — you care so deeply that you want it to be *just right*. But perfectionism is just fear. You are afraid of putting an unfamiliar or unknown part of yourself out to the world. The same with procrastination; it's another expression of fear. You are afraid of doing something, and so you find all sorts of other things that need to be done and then *oopsie...* you ran out of time.

I could write an entire book about fear. But what is important for the understanding of the 20% Power Principle of Discomfort is that fear will necessarily be a part of your 20% discomfort. And as you will soon see, you have the power to decide what role it plays in your life. Yet, nothing happens until you own your fears, thoughts, and everything else that comes with them.

 # OWN IT TO GET OVER IT

You have the ability to accept or decline a thought. You have the ability to stop a thought that will keep you small and change it to one that empowers you. It's your superpower *but* you must take that control. For some people, emotional turmoil will prevent them from changing their thoughts, and those are real and serious disorders that you should work through with a professional. But for the majority of us, owning our thoughts is just a matter of making a decision: if I created this thought, I can just as easily create another one. At first this will be hard, just like it was hard for me to make the path after the snowstorm, but once you repeat that thought often enough, you will condition it. In fact, our brains physically change with repetition. It's the same with the rest of your body. You don't leave your first day back in the gym with bicep guns. But go diligently and a transformation of your body is inevitable. The tricky things here are emotions. They might make it more or less of an effort to control your thoughts, so just remember emotions pass. They are a response to a trigger, and they are temporary. Flow with the emotion and when on the other side, go back and become aware of your thoughts because ultimately you own them. However, we often confuse our thoughts with our circumstances.

"Oh Cristina, you don't understand. If only you had the same childhood that I had, then your thoughts would be different. Or, if only you had experienced this or that, then you would understand that I cannot help but to think that."

I HEAR you; I really do. But I want to challenge you. I don't believe that just because I was able to overcome something that someone should be able to overcome that same thing in the same way. A good coach doesn't tell what to do, they present you tools and guide you as you choose which tools you resonate with and can grab onto. We are all different. But we also have power to change. One of the clearest examples of this, for me, is author Viktor Frankl in his book *Man's Search for Meaning* (1946). Dr. Frankl, who was a psychiatrist imprisoned at Auschwitz, the horrific concentration camp of Nazi Germany, writes about the discovery of his theory of logotherapy. In his moving account, he states that when you cannot change a situation, the only thing you can change is yourself. He couldn't change the fact that he was a prisoner living harrowing experiences, so he changed his thoughts and his perception of his life and its meaning.

Now, this is complicated and potentially dangerous territory with victims of crime and trauma; I am not a certified, trauma-informed therapist. I am sharing my personal view of the world which has come to life through years of working with adults and children alike. But if Viktor Frankel was able to change his thoughts to empower himself and survive a concentration camp, then I think there is hope for all of us.

As I mentioned before, when Joe died, I turned to books. I thought they would give me a nice, linear roadmap of what would unfold as I navigated my first year as a widow. I was wrong and I hated all of those books, with few exceptions. I also joined a lot of grief-based Facebook groups and discovered that grief is a very personal and individual journey, so I don't judge people on how they process their experience, but I personally didn't relate to those groups.

I read comments such as: "I can't live without him," "My life is over," and "It's been five years and I miss him just as much as I did in year one." And my gut reaction was *Oh, hell no. I don't want that to be my story.* I loved my husband with everything that I am, I still do. But I was also well aware that though our life together had come to an end, at least in its physical sense, I was still alive.

When I got sober, I had to restart. I went to daily Alcoholics Anonymous meetings, met all sorts of people, and did a lot of deep personal work. I was recreating myself as a woman who didn't drink, and that was difficult because I didn't know how to be that woman. I realized becoming a woman who doesn't drink and becoming a widow have followed similar patterns. Getting sober, I could've chosen the story of 'damaged goods.' "Who would ever love me now that I had been in a mental institution and can't go to a happy hour?"

Or I could choose another story: "Wow, I am surrounded by people who really understand me and who have the same scars that I do. I am a badass for surviving my own destructive actions. I am not damaged goods. On the contrary, you want me on your team because I know how to come back."

I chose the latter which allowed me to become my own person, marry Joe, have our boys and—quite frankly—live a pretty wonderful life, even if it didn't include any happy hours. Today, I am not the person I was before I met Joe, but I am also not the person I was as Joe's wife. As I continue to rediscover myself, I can choose the story I tell.

You don't have to wait to be in rehab, or lose your husband, to change the narrative your life. You can do it right now.

AGAIN, IT might feel strange at first, but have you ever seen a toddler take their first steps? They are awkward too, and then before you know it, they are running. It's the same with you and your thoughts. But you have to own the narrative. You need to take responsibility for your thoughts, as well as your other superpowers, in order to change anything about your life. Otherwise, you will continue blaming your circumstances, other people, or your environment. You will focus your attention on the reasons why you can't be something or the other, instead of looking for the opportunities to change. Blaming is extraordinarily disempowering because you will think you are stuck.

For example, if you think it is your parents' fault that you lack confidence because they said you'd never be successful, you will spend your days proving them wrong or proving them right. It's about them; not you. If you think your parents, though misguided, did the best they could, you release the power they have on your ultimate success and can build a new story. You are no longer at their mercy. I am here to tell you that you can take control of your thoughts, and this starts with taking ownership of them. This is not to say the others might not have hurt you or done you wrong; taking ownership of your thoughts does not equal forgiveness. Taking ownership is setting a boundary that signals, "You told me I'd never be successful, and when I didn't know better I believed you and thought I would never succeed at anything I did. I can't control you or what you said, but I can control how I think about this, and today I chose to think I can succeed in whatever the heck I want." Ownership is empowerment, releasing blame is understanding that though you might have been the victim of a circumstance, you don't have to think you are a victim of your life.

··

Taking ownership of your thoughts
does not equal forgiveness.

··

ONE FINAL note on owning your thoughts: Everyone has a story that reinforces their identity whether that story propels us towards our goals or keeps us stuck. The trick is, everyone has it, but only *you* get to tell yours. When you tell the story of your life, to yourself or to others, you are actually telling *your* version of the story. You think from your point of view. I'm sure if you asked my parents the story of my early sobriety, they'd probably focus on different things. They would tell you *their* story of what happened to me from *their* perspective. And though the event itself is the same, the three of us experienced it very differently. Your story is yours to own and you can change the lens you see it through.

THINGS DON'T HAPPEN
FOR A REASON

IF YOU would've told me in the thick of my grief that things happen for a reason, I might've cursed you. What would possibly be a good reason to take my husband and leave my boys without their dad? I can accept the fact, but I get to choose the meaning.

Things happen. You give it a reason.

I KNOW some religious traditions might disagree, but that is how I think (see what I just did there?). Bad things happen to good people, unfathomable atrocities are committed, crimes are perpetrated every day. What any of these events mean, in the grand scheme of things, is entirely up to you. Just like Frankl made his experience in a concentration camp mean something different than just being tortured day in and day out, you can too. And when you are stuck, or you just don't know what it means, here is a tool for you. It starts with a legend I tell all my students, adults, and kids alike.

Once upon a time, there was an old man who had a horse, and he relied on that horse to work his field so he could feed his family. One day, the horse ran away. And so, the whole village was very concerned for this man. They ran up to him and lamented, "Oh old man! Isn't this terrible? You no longer have a horse to plow your fields, you're going to starve. What a disaster. The Gods must be punishing you."

To which the old man simple replied, "It remains to be seen."

The next day, the horse came back with another horse, a very powerful horse that could do twice the amount of work in the field. And the villagers were so happy for the old man! "Oh, old man! You are so lucky! Now you have two horses to work the fields. What a blessing. The Gods are looking down on you with favor."

And the old wise man just said: "It remains to be seen."

A few days later, the old man's son was riding the new horse, and he fell and broke his leg. And once again, the villagers were very concerned, and they cried to the old man over terrible news. "Your son had such a terrible fall, and now he's crippled. What a terrible thing. He can no longer help you plow the field."

To which the old man replied...you guessed it, "It remains to be seen."

A few months later, war broke out, and the army came to the village, and took all the young men to fight as soldiers. But the old man's son couldn't go because he was crippled. And the villagers were so happy for him.

Still, he replied, "It remains to be seen."

THIS CAN go on and on, but you get the idea. Things *don't* happen for a reason. Things happen, *you give them meaning.* Joe's death happened because his body produced cancerous cells which attacked his kidney and travelled to his heart. I can go with that thought, or I can think he is paying for a sin committed in a past life, or that one of his nurses had to feel our love for each other to run back and say yes to the man who proposed to her, or I can make it mean that life sucks and then you die. All of these options are available. Both you and I have choice.

Thinking things happen for a reason, is disempowering. It's life happening *to* me. I for one, don't want to be a victim of my life, I prefer to lead it.

But I often don't know why something is happening, so I reframe that as "it remains to be seen." That is forward thinking; it's empowering. Life stays open for what happens next, and I can take actions to influence the future. The beauty of "it remains to be seen" is that it's neutral, neither positive nor negative. This allows us balance. When things are going really well, we stay humble because we don't know what is around the corner. But when things are rough, it gives us hope, because there's a chance they can turn around. Life has inevitable ups and downs, if we just embrace that, it'll make the journey a whole lot smoother.

Joe's death wasn't the end of my story, it was the end of what might be the most important chapter. But I am still here, and as long as I live, life will happen, and new chapters will be written. I prefer to be its author.

 # ZOOM OUT AND CHILL OUT

ANOTHER CHANGE of perspective tool to help with your superpower of thoughts is what I call "Zoom Out." Here's a story that illustrates it.

In the spring after Joe's death, the boys and I went to Copper Mountain, Colorado for the USASA National Snowboard Championships. This would be the end of what I labeled *the difficult season.*

I WORKED a little, rode a little, and supported the boys in their competitions a lot. On my last run of the difficult season, I decided I would go all the way up the mountain and make it down calmly strengthening my gratitude muscles with some of the tools I will show you in Chapter 6. I went up the American Eagle lift which sits six people, but when I hopped on there was only one other man sharing the chair with me. I don't love the feeling of dangling in the air on the lift, so the first thing I did as the chairlift started moving was to bring the safety bar down, and that's when it all started.

"Do you mind if I put this down?" It was a rhetorical question.

"Yes," he said. "Leave it up."

"I really prefer to bring it down, I am afraid of heights."

"Then you shouldn't be here," he replied.

I was taken back. There is the flight, fight, or freeze response to stress. I am decidedly a freeze kind of girl. In fact, it is a joke amongst my family that I have great comebacks to these types of situations...except that I have them three days later.

I couldn't just bring the safety bar down as it would hit his head, and here we were floating thirty feet from the ground for two miles. I was frozen on that chairlift experiencing my biggest trigger: *powerlessness*.

I was quiet with my thoughts: *What an idiot. Does he not know this is my last run of the season, that this season has been very difficult?* And all of a sudden, I blurted out of nowhere: "Can we please put the bar down, my husband died."

He yelled back at me: "What does that have to do with anything? He probably shot himself to get away from you, you stupid B**** C**** If you need to put the bar down, you shouldn't be here."

And on and on this man berated me for the fifteen minutes the chair lift took to get to the top. I felt trapped. I couldn't jump off, I was afraid I was going to fall off, and this man was losing his mind.

I got off the lift and was shaking. As I started my ride down, I'd fall every few feet. This was not the way my last run was supposed to be. This was not the way my *life* was supposed to be. I was not supposed to be a widow and single mom. I sat on the snow in the sun and calmed myself down. I was *not* going to let some idiot ruin my last run of the difficult season.

But try as I might, I kept falling. I was crying, I was frazzled, and he was winning. So, I sat down again. And I began to "zoom out." I took a wider view.

Something terrible must have happened to make that man so miserable and so abusive to a complete stranger. Maybe his wife just told him she wanted a divorce that morning (frankly I wouldn't have blamed her), or perhaps there was some sort of PTSD issue, or maybe his parents didn't love him when he was a child. I don't know his story, but I know he had one.

I made it up. An entire life story about how he had an accident and had a brain injury and his wife left him and I began zooming out of the lift ride. And something incredible happened, the more I zoomed out, the more compassion I had for him.

I had no idea who he was or what his story really was, but it didn't matter. This wasn't about him; it was about me. *I* was feeling better. I finished the run, got back on the lift and did it again, even if it meant I would be late to lunch. I went up, this time alone in the six-seat lift, I lowered the safety bar, enjoyed the view, breathed in the fresh air, and tried not to think about the man who had verbally assaulted me half hour earlier. I rode down and it was magical. It was just what I needed to close the difficult season.

And as soon as I got down, it all came back to me. Compassion be damned. The anger, the powerlessness of being stuck in a chair lift thirty feet high without a safety bar with a complete lunatic of a man insulting me. I went to the administration office and reported him. I told Mountain Operations what happened, what he was wearing, what time I was on the lift, and they sent an alert that if he was recognized he would be escorted out of the mountain. I did it because I didn't want someone else to go through what I had gone through. But also because it helped me feel empowered. I have no idea if he was found or what happened to him. But I know how I felt, and I've been teaching this zooming out technique ever since.

I can zoom out and switch anger to compassion. I can forgive him not because he was right, but because it would help me enjoy the last day of the difficult season. I was not owning his 20% of discomfort, but I owned mine.

Therefore, when you feel the discomfort, know you have the power to create a story about it, to give it meaning. What story do you want to have? If your discomfort is that you hate your job, you have the power to choose thoughts around it: "My job sucks and I suck" or "My job sucks, I deserve better." Both options are available to you, and they live in you to the extent that you allow those thoughts. And here is the empowering, awesome news: *If you own them, you can change them.* You get to decide which thoughts are helping you move forward, and which ones are keeping you stuck. And you get to choose what to *do* with them.

I TOTALLY understand if you think this is a Lalaland tool where you create an alternate reality just to feel better. And you'd be right. But here is the deal. Where does this alternate reality live? Yep, in your thoughts. And who owns your thoughts? Right again, you. So, who cares? If I told you that I am creating a parallel universe where I am a gazillionaire and rent a private jet to go to the corner meanwhile my bank account is empty, that is me not living in the real world. But when you are faced with a situation over which you are powerless, why not calm yourself down by fueling compassion instead of anger? In fact, isn't that what mediation is about, to get you out of your reality? Give it a try before you toss this tool out.

Sometimes, there are negative thoughts that pop up that we didn't even know we had, because they were buried deep in our subconscious. While that is true, I classify these as beliefs. Beliefs are thoughts that you have repeated and accepted as truth, and there is a lot we can do to uncover and change those into *empowering* beliefs. But we can't get there without talking about words because *words are thoughts expressed.*

Samantha's Story

I met Samantha in the summer of 2020. She had been furloughed from her job as a restaurant manager due to the pandemic, and stayed home with her three children as the world shut down. During that time, Samantha realized just how much of their lives she was missing. Her discomfort was enough to motivate her to take action and find a way to stay home with her kiddos once the lockdown was over. She told me she was giving herself two years to quit her job and work for herself. "Two years! That's half the life of your youngest son. You want to wait that long to take a more active role in his life?" She thought I was crazy; she had moved up the ranks in the same restaurant for the past twenty years, surely it couldn't be so easy to just change careers.

That's the thing. "Leaving my job will be difficult," was Samantha's repetitive thought based on her life experience. There is nothing wrong with that, unless that thought keeps you stuck in your discomfort. Samantha wanted a change, and it would necessarily require courage to leave her employer of twenty years. Of course, there is a risk with leaving your job and starting a business. That is what she focused on. Her negative bias kept her in the thought loop of all the things that could possibly go wrong. Her business might not be successful for a while, she was starting from scratch, what if no one signed up for her programs? There was plenty to worry about. Those were the issues facing that version of Samantha – the employee of twenty years.

Together, we used the same zoom out tool I taught you in this chapter. When Samantha took a few steps back and saw the whole of her life, she began to see there was more to the decision than just her bank account. How would she feel about herself leaving her kids every day when she knew she wanted to be with them? Was she setting the example that when things are too scary, stay where you are? There is also a risk of not following your heart, and not being where you want to be, in this case at home with her kids.

By zooming out, Samantha was able to realign her thoughts about what was a priority. Once she decided it was to stay home, then the answers of how to do that began to show up. She still had doubts about her abilities, but she knew those were skills she could learn. Fear was still present, but she didn't let that stop her. Do you know how long it took Samantha to give her two weeks' notice to the restaurant that employed her for twenty years? Less than eight weeks.

Today, Samantha owns a successful children's fitness business. She grew so fast, it was now her business infringing on family time. There is still discomfort, but her life container is bigger. Plus, this version of Samantha – the empowered business owner – is able to make the new decisions necessary to handle her new discomfort. I don't know about you, but I'd rather have the discomfort of my business being too successful than my job is keeping me away from my kids.

4.

THE POWER OF WORDS

WORDS BECOME
SELF-FULFILLING PROPHECIES

THE WORDS you choose to use are your second superpower. They provide the easiest way to understand your thoughts because all you have to do is listen. I mean *really* listen. You are who you say you are. Your life is what you say it is. Your words are the way you communicate your thoughts and ideas. And many of us have ideas we don't even know are there!

Let's start our discussion with two of the most important words in any language: "I am." Whatever you put after it will be true. I am smart, I am capable, I am brave, or I am a failure, I am a coward, I am shy. The real truth, however, is that we are all a little bit of everything. But whatever words you use to describe yourself *most* of the time, that is your identity. Here's a little story that shows you just how deep and transformative this concept of identity is.

In HIGH school, you would be more likely to find me behind the gym smoking pot than doing anything *inside* the gym. When my sons were born, I wanted to be an active mom who did things with them. But physically, I couldn't run around the block without gasping for air. So, one day, when the boys were just toddlers, I decided to run a 5K (3.1 miles) race in my neighborhood.

Oh. My. God.

At the finish line, you would've thought I won an Olympic medal by the way I felt. Me? The super-overweight and exhausted mom of two boys under two? Me? The pack-a-day smoker for twenty years? I ran a 5K?

Woah—

And if I did that, what else could I do? It was that feeling of empowerment that became my new high, and I chased it with gusto. I went from 5Ks to 10Ks, and from half-marathons to triathlons, and from Ironman triathlons to racing triathlons pulling a quadriplegic friend, and more. I was always challenging myself physically to see what else I could do.

But the identity of the girl in the back of the gym stayed with me even as my body changed. So much so, that when it came to my first Ironman triathlon, I almost didn't sign in. Ironman is a long race: 2.4-mile swim, 112 miles on the bike, and then you run 26.2 miles—a marathon. You cannot wing it. To get to Ironman, and to complete the race, you need to train. It's usually a yearlong preparation, demanding a huge commitment of time, energy, and money. Joe was incredibly supportive and had daddy time with the boys on the weekends while I hit the pavement for hours on end.

My first Ironman was in November of 2013, in Panama City Beach, Florida.

There is a lot to do before the race including checking your bike into 'transition.' This is a heavily secured area where athletes leave their bikes overnight. I was hyped and nervous because the next time I saw my bike would be at the race itself. Everyone around me looked very fit, and very serious. I felt more like a whale, sausaged into a tight triathlon suit. Therefore, when I approached the entrance of transition and heard the security officer call "Athletes only," I almost turned around and went the other way. It didn't occur to me that "athletes" included me.

I mean, who was I kidding? I had spent the last ten years on the couch, and the last four either having babies or taking care of them. As I turned around to leave, I realized: "Wait! He is talking about me!" My arms had my race number tattooed on them, and my bike had two stickers that clearly matched the number on my arms. Yes, that was me, and at that moment I became an athlete. Not only was I an athlete, but if I ever finished that race, I would become an Ironman triathlete.

I finished Ironman Florida, and two others.

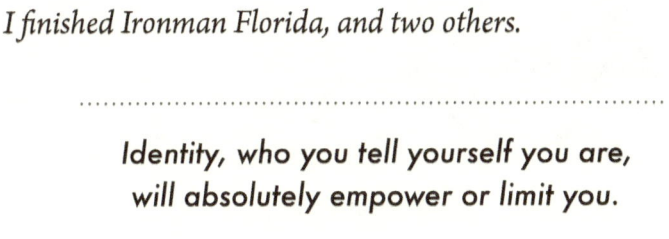

Identity, who you tell yourself you are, will absolutely empower or limit you.

IDENTITIES ARE complicated, yet we tend to describe ourselves with words given to us by our parents, teachers, and friends. We also have an identity based on what we do, and together they make up who we are. For example: I am a mother, a widow, and an entrepreneur. I am also caring, ambitious, and a risk taker. In the same breath I can also tell you I am fearful and indecisive. Some of these words put forth my highest self, and others my lowest. But who I really am, is the identity I choose to live in the most. *We* get to choose which words used by others we accept, and even more, we choose what words to use to describe ourselves. And the superpower of words is that they will influence our beliefs about ourselves and therefore our actions and results.

My first 5k in Key Biscayne, Florida. I felt like I won the olympics.

AWARENESS IS THE ROOT
OF ALL CHANGE

WE CANNOT talk about *words* without speaking of *awareness*. I don't know about you, but sometimes I open my mouth and out comes my mother. Not my words, but her words. Because I heard them so often, they were ingrained in me. They live somewhere deep in my subconscious and influence my thoughts. But ultimately, as we saw previously, I am in control of both my superpowers: thoughts and words. The trick is sometimes we think and say things, and we don't even know why or where they came from. It doesn't mean that you are weak, it just means that you are not as aware as you could be to your unconscious motivations. Even the most attuned and aware of people still stumble on this.

Awareness happens after the thought is expressed either internally or externally in words you speak to someone else.

THE GOAL is to become as *internally* aware as possible, because while words remain in your head, you still own them. Once words are spoken to someone else, those words own you, and all you can do is accept the consequences, and if necessary, ask for forgiveness.

I cannot tell you how many times I have yelled at my kids in frustration or anger. If you ask them, they'll likely tell you, "Yeah, my mom is a yeller." I hate when that happens. But I am only human, and it still happens more often than I'd like to admit. I get caught in moment and out of my mouth come words that I would've rather not have shared. Things like, "Why can't you just x-y-z? You *always* do yada-yada! I am not your maid." Or the worst one: "Who do you think you are to blah blah blah?"

Ugh. I cringe just thinking about it. Yet, I share this with you so that you can be aware when it happens to you. And if you hear yourself saying things you don't want to, whether that is yelling at your kid or gossiping about a co-worker, learn from it, grow from it, and own it, so that with practice and with tools, you can change it.

Awareness by itself won't bring change. But awareness is the first step toward avoiding our tendency to blurt out words we may later regret. And just so you know, you tend to use the most needling words on people who are closest to you. Chances are that if a waiter takes a long time to bring you food, you are not going to tell him off. But if it's your partner, child, or sibling who is taking an extra-long time to bring you that glass of water you asked for a million years ago… you might. You know these people love you, therefore you drop down your guard, become less aware and out comes the venom.

So, how do you cultivate awareness? Ugh. It's hard. It requires you to pay attention and be more deliberate in what you say to yourself and others. You need to be vigilant. I had a client, let's call her Sue, who would constantly refer to herself as a "dumbass." She said it so often, she wasn't even aware of how much she used that word. When I called her out on it, she was a little resentful, but she hired me to empower her not to be her buddy. I asked for permission to point out to her every time she called herself a dumbass to which she agreed. It was irritating for both of us, but all it took was a one-hour group coaching call for her, and her peers, to realize just how much she reinforced the dumbass identity by not being aware of her words. Awareness is a practice, a habit. You'll never be aware 24x7, but you can have a focused intention for a limited amount of time. Although Sue got the memo during that call, this was going to be a hard habit to break. Therefore, I suggested that every day, she pick one activity where others were involved, to cultivate awareness of her words. One day it was dinner, another day a business meeting, another time coffee. Can you guess what happened? Catching herself became easier and easier until the habit of calling herself a dumbass broke.

We all mess up and say words we don't mean. When that happens, we feel ... drumroll ... discomfort. Discomfort is the clue, a sign, feedback that there is something there you have to deal with. Welcome it, pay attention to it, recognize it, and tell yourself, "In the past I... but now I..."

Let's say that your best friend is coming to your neck of the woods and asks you to meet her for lunch. You have half an hour, and you tell her so. On the day, you are excited to meet her and go out of your way to arrange your work schedule so that you are on time. You have been sitting there for ten minutes waiting, when she comes into the restaurant. For the last ten minutes you have been stewing in your thoughts: *Why does she do this? Didn't I tell her to be on time? Now we need to be rushed for lunch and that usually gives me heartburn. Ugh, I love her, but she is so inconsiderate.* And on and on your thoughts go. So, when she sits down and apologizes for being late, you give her a piece of your mind because you have been ruminating about her tardiness for some time. Then you learn she was late because she was helping a little old lady who was lost, and that caused her to miss her train forcing her to take a cab instead and there was traffic. You feel like a shmuck for telling her off. Right then and there, just think to yourself:

> *In the past, I would lash out at people, but now I know better, and I am changing that behavior.*
> *In the past, I was stingy with my family because I was afraid of running out of money, but now I am working on my money story, and I don't have to do that anymore.*
> *In the past, I broke a diet almost as soon as I started it, but now I am committed to my health and know there are better ways, and I am adopting better habits to help me with this.*

THIS WILL help you reinforce that you are on a path of change and empowerment. And it will also help give yourself some grace when you inevitably mess up. However, this will only be possible if you pay attention.

With the people closest to you, be open about your desire to change, and they will be more than willing to point out to you the words they hear. For example, my kids once asked me why I always said "no" to everything. If they asked for something, I replied no, even though I didn't really *mean* no. It was a conditioned response. So, I made it fun. I told them I say no because it just flows out easier from my mouth than yes. "Nooooooo…" Smooth, isn't it? We made a rule that if I said no, they could ask again, but only twice more. After that, it was a definitive no. If I said no three times, then we could agree that it wasn't a reflex, but a decision. The practice really helped me pause on the whole "unconscious no" reaction, and the boys helped me realize just how often I did it. Meanwhile, since I gave them permission to ask again, it triggered a pause where I could actually *think* about my answer instead of blurting it out opening up the space for dialogue.

"Can I go to Johnny's house?"
"No." (Immediate response.)
"Why?"
"I don't know. Let me think about it."
"Yeah no."
"Why?"
"Because it is late, and you still have to do homework."

THIS LITTLE practice not only helped me recognize the pattern I had of just saying no, but it gave me space to think about the appropriate answer. Meanwhile, my kids understood that no means no, after the third time, for real.

SEVEN PHRASES TO CHANGE YOUR LIFE

IF WORDS are a superpower, then these seven phrases are the fuel. The first set of three phrases empower you to change your attitude about anything. Let's start with "I have to," "I want to," and "I choose to."

1. "I have to..."

"I have to" suggests duty, obligation, or something that might be a burden: I *have* to do something; I *have* to feed my kids; I *have* to take the dog for the walk; I *have* to earn money. "I have to" phrases are demands that external forces have put on you and keep you in a powerless state. "I have to" is mandated by someone else. But what if you were to change from, for example, "I have to find a job" to "I want to find a job?" That feels a little more empowering don't you think?

You might gag a little because maybe you feel like you *don't* want to find a job, but you have to. And if this is you, then just follow the thought. Why do you have to find a job? Probably to pay your bills, to have a sense of independence, to do whatever you want with the money you earned, to use that money from the job to fund a passion project, etc. There are many reasons why people want to get jobs, and you might relate to one of those. How would it sound now?

2. "I want to..."

"I want to get a job so I can..." Better? Probably feels a little more empowering, yet the only problem with "I want" is that it places whatever it is you desire in the future. So, your sneaky negative self can say "I want to get a job because I want to take my family on vacation...*Because* right now I have a shitty job that pays peanuts, and I am not good enough to get a different job and blah-blah-blah down the spiral you go. Let's shift that.

3. "I choose to..."

So, what if we use the third variation: "I choose to." "I choose to get a job because I want to take my family on vacation." Now you are using empowering words that bring the action to the present. "I choose" focuses on today. "I want" focuses on tomorrow. You could choose not to get a new job, but because you want to take your family on vacation you choose to have your empowered self show up to the interview instead of *having* to do it.

The truth is that either way you slice it, the need to get a job is still there regardless of what you think about it. But you can empower yourself with your words or continue to use words that will keep you a victim of your circumstance. Which words do you choose?

"Really, Cristina? Like that is going to make such a big difference."

ABSO-FREAKIN'-LUTELY. The more you tell yourself that you are *choosing* versus *having* to do something, the more that thought becomes embedded in your brain. Remember the neural pathways we talked about. Your brain also looks for efficiency. Once it accepts a fact and knows it, it just stores it, and moves on, opening the capacity to learn new things.

A little note about choice. You are always making a choice. Even if you are not *actively* choosing, that's still a decision. Not choosing a candidate in an election, and not voting are choices. Not going to the doctor when you are sick is a choice. In addition, either you make the choice, or the choice is made for you. If you have a little leak in your roof and you choose not to do anything about it because it's small, eventually, it will get big enough that you will not have a choice but to fix it. I also teach this to my students and it's especially poignant for the older ones.

ON THE first day of class, I ask everyone to introduce themselves with their name and their favorite potato chip. I usually get a couple of answers: Fritos, Takis, Lays Limon (my personal favorite) but I also get a bunch of "I don't know," "anything," and "I don't care." Those last ones often think they are funny. Or, they might be thinking, "What does it matter?"

What they don't know is that I go to the store before the next class and get them whatever they told me. So, I buy the Fritos, Takis and Lays. For the others, who didn't express a preference, I buy them whatever is on sale, usually pork rinds. On the second class, I give everyone what they told me was their favorite, and the pork rinds to the others.

I explain: "I was here to help you and give you whatever it is you wanted. But if you don't tell me what you want, if you don't make a choice, I can't give it to you. And most importantly, if you don't tell me what you want, I will give you what is best for *me* not for *you*. I gave you what was on sale so that I spent less money. That serves me more than it serves you. But I was willing to give you whatever potato chip you wanted. All you had to do is make a decision about which potato chip you liked the most."

Now, IF you want to take your word choice to the next level, I have an even better one for you. We saw "I have to," "I want to," and "I choose to," but let me introduce to you the GOAT in the personal development world: *Gratitude*. We'll talk much more about this in Chapter 6. But the fourth phrase to change your life is: "I get to." I am grateful that *I get to...*

4. I get to...

You might say: "I get to find a job, I am smart, and I am capable, I have skills that someone will value, I am able to work, I get to then take my family on vacation and I get to explore a new part of the world with them..."

Think about how often you use the words "I get to." I am guessing not too often. But if you become deliberate, I promise you, your thoughts will shift to more empowered ones. Here's an example. When I first began coaching clients, I was unsure of myself. So, if a client was struggling with something, instead of going into default freakout mode thinking I sucked, I'd go to "I get to." Because Jane is having a really hard time with believing she can start a business, "I get to" find a new way of connecting her to her dream; of teaching a concept; of helping her at a deeper level. "I get to" helps leave fear behind and allows us to look for what could be good about this situation. "I get to" takes practice, but it's well worth the effort.

THE NEXT three phrases that will change your life have to do with emotional integration, a huge topic we won't dive deeply into here. However, there are two important things to know about emotions that we did not cover earlier. First is, just because you have an intense emotional response to something does not mean it is indeed true. Feelings aren't facts. When I was younger, I would imagine the worst possible case scenario for everything. So, if I saw a lost dog, I wouldn't just think, "That's a lost dog. Let me see if I can help." I would think, "That poor dog. The owner must have dumped it. It feels sad, abandoned, and unloved." I would then enter the realm of my make-believe sad world and would end up in tears projecting onto this dog any feelings of unworthiness or abandonment I had. But just because I *felt* that didn't mean it was true. For all I know the dog comes from a loving home and happened to go on an adventure, much to the heartache of his owner, just like my dogs have done in the past. The whole sad story that brought me to tears, was never real.

The second thing to note about emotions is that feelings pass. I experience grief as tidal waves of extraordinary sadness and even despair. When it hits, I literally bend over in pain and find it hard to breathe. I cover my face and prefer to go hide somewhere, so I can let it flow through me. That's the thing. I *allow* the feeling, because at that moment the grief is real as I hit the floor crying. But I also know it will pass. And when it passes, then I can pick myself up, but while I am in it, I must surrender to the emotion. I have noticed that, over time, these waves are just as intense, but they don't come as often. Knowing that whatever emotion you are feeling, positive or negative, will pass is a gift. It is much easier to allow emotions when you know you there will be an end to them. Here are the next three phrases that will change your life.

....

Feelings aren't fact, and they don't last forever either.

....

5. "I am..."

Let's use sadness as an example, since we just saw what grief feels like to me. If I say, "I am sad," what I am saying is that *my identity is sadness.* Every cell in me is sadness, I am nothing but sad. I can't see or be anything but sad. That is a disempowered view of myself because it defines me as something that hurts. Plus, it's not true. I am more than my grief and sadness.

6. "I feel..."

If I say, "I feel sadness," now I take the feeling from inside of me and place it outside. Sadness is not *who* I am, but it is an emotion that I am feeling or experiencing at the moment. The ability to do this is a game-changer, because it allows you to have a view beyond the emotion. It's as if there is a spectrum of feelings or emotions that I have access to. *One of them* is sadness. And that is the one I am interacting with right now; it does not define the entirety of who I am.

7. "There is..."

And finally, the ninja level phrase: "*There is* sadness." I admit, I find this one difficult, but when I am able to work with these words, they give me the largest sense of control and empowerment. Sadness, as we just saw, is one of the feelings I have access to. I acknowledge that sadness may be knocking and asking me to play, but I have the power to decide when to allow it and when not to. It's feedback. It tells me, "Hey, pay attention to me there is something here." Sometimes I let it in, I feel it, I cry. Other times, I acknowledge it with "Oh wow, this situation brings up emotion. There is sadness here. That's interesting." But I can leave it there. I don't have to go into the pain and experience it. Not because I am shutting it out or pushing it down, but maybe I am not in the mood to go on the roller coaster that sadness takes me on, and it is not at such an overpowering level that I have no choice but to succumb to it. I am not afraid of feeling sadness, but at that point I can understand *there is sadness*, and I can ask, "What caused it to come up? Why now? Why in this situation?" The amount of internal awareness you get from this is immense. Next time an emotion pops up that you are not entangled with, try it. Say "*There is* sadness, anger, resentment, fear…" Allow yourself to wonder what that is all about while exploring it with curiosity.

FIVE WORDS THAT DEFINE YOU

ANOTHER USEFUL exercise to do around words is one I call "Top Five." I am going to ask you a series of questions. Just answer the first words that come to your head. Don't judge it, don't worry. Allow yourself to be impulsive, these tend to be our most honest answers. To get ready, divide a sheet of paper into five columns. I've numbered each stage of this exercise to match the columns where you will complete them.

1. In the first column, before you think too much, write down the first five *adjectives* you use to describe yourself. No filter, no worry, no judgement. Do it, right now. Just the first five words. Once you have written them down, go back and make sure they are adjectives. Many times, as we saw before, we describe ourselves by nouns, or by what we do. Those are definitely a part of our identity. But here, we are looking for who you are. For example: I could describe myself as: mother, entrepreneur, widow. But those are nouns. That is not what we are looking for. Here are some adjectives in case you struggled with this:

Wise, Empathic, Enthusiastic, Fair, Modest, Grateful, Ambitious, Athletic, Optimistic, Artistic, Honest, Kind, Brave, Creative, Disciplined, Independent, Curious, Open-minded,

Compassionate, Cooperative, Flexible, Funny, Confident, Assertive, Persistent, Aware, Thoughtful, Caring, Decisive, Forgiving, Patient, Spiritual, Intelligent, Logical, Adventurous, Healthy, Abundant...

2. Now, I want you to think of someone you admire. It can be someone you know in person, a famous celebrity, a historical figure—it doesn't matter. Think of that person, and in column two, write down at least five words to describe that person. Do that now before you read ahead.

3. For column three, think of another person you admire, just as above. Write at least five words for that person. Why are they on your list? What makes them special? What qualities do they show the world? Same thing, complete this person before moving on to the next column.

4. For column four, think of someone else you admire. Past or present, it doesn't matter. I think you know what to do by now. Complete your third person before continuing.

....

What you admire in someone else is something you have in you.

....

Here's the thing: what you admire in someone else is something you already have in you. Whether you consciously know it or not, that is a different story, but you recognize in others what you have in yourself. For example, when I first did this exercise, I realized a couple of people on my list were very creative and very good with words. That is because I value those traits, otherwise I wouldn't have picked those people. My client Kathy had a completely different list of people, two in the medical field, and one a researcher. She valued traits that were related to thoroughness, data, and logic. There is no way any of those words would be on any of my lists. Therefore, trust that the people you chose represent qualities that are important for you and that you recognize, even if just a tiny bit, in yourself.

5. Next, for column five, look at all the words on the page. If someone who knew you well was going to describe you, which five words on the page would they use? Write those in column five. Now, are there any words that are in *both* column one and in column five? Sometimes we don't recognize our strengths because we assume everyone has them, but it's just not true. When we ask how someone else would view you, it helps us expand the perception of who we are.

FINALLY, LOOK at all the words on your page. Circle any words that repeat themselves (hint: those are important to you) and choose five words that you either currently admire in yourself or aspire to have more of if you are not there yet.

Those five words are your *Power Words*, positive words that are deliberate and that are in you, perhaps not to the extent that you want them to be, but they are who you are. Now that you know them, it's time to put them to use. From now on, be very conscious of the words that you use to describe yourself. If for example, you're talking to a friend, and say, "Ugh, I can't believe I did that, I'm such a dumbass I totally forgot about blah-blah-blah," then catch yourself. Remember our discussion on awareness? Bring that back; change the narrative. "No, I'm not a dumbass. I'm actually very good at this. But I was just busy. And this slipped my mind. Human error. It happens." While you're at it, let go of self-deprecating humor. That is not helpful either; we think it's funny to make fun of ourselves, but all we're doing is reinforcing that old identity, instead of integrating our new Power Words.

You are your own biggest critic, but that's a choice. You don't have to be. Why not be your biggest cheerleader instead? Why pull yourself down? I don't know what your story is, but I know that you can change it. And using those Power Words is a great first step. Remember only *you* can control your thoughts.

And here is a final instruction: Do not speak to yourself, or do not think to yourself, or of yourself in a way that you wouldn't to a child. You would not tell a child "You are such a dumbass," "Your butt is too big," or "I wish you were smarter." Imagine how hurt that child would be. Well, my friend, that is what you are doing to yourself. You might be rolling your eyes at me right now, perhaps thinking I should lighten up. However, I have worked with enough people to know that what you practice you make permanent. And if you want to feel better about yourself and overcome your current discomfort you have to be vigilant about the words you use.

"No Cristina, you don't understand.
I really am these negative things and using Power Words
seems like Lalaland positive bullshit."

IN MY EmpowerFit Curriculum, the first lesson we teach
children is to use Power Words. In school, children are
taught to be nice, kind, a good friend, etc. We tell them
that in the field, we want them to use Power Words such
as *strong, brave, mighty,* and *fierce.* Then we have a relay race
where children have to run, pick up a ball and shout their
power word when they return the ball. The next person in
the relay must run and collect the next ball and shout their
power word as loudly as possible when they return. One
of the things I find fascinating is how at first, some kids are
reluctant to shout out their words. However, the distances
increase with each round, and it becomes more and more
tiring. By the end, the children are really pushing themselves
to complete the game. And as the game gets harder, as they
get more tired, they shout their Power Words louder and
louder. Maybe what you can do to become your words is
to commit to working on your discomfort, and when you
need to push through, use your Power Words just like the
kids do in the field.

I understand. You are not perfect. Nor am I. Are there
things we do that are less than ideal? Do we make bad
decisions? Are there aspects of ourselves that are not the
most flattering and we would like to change? Of course,
there are! And these reside in our 20% of discomfort. But
let's put them in their right place and give them their right

weight. They are not all of who you are, so train yourself to find your strengths. That is where our beliefs come in.

Shayna's Story

I COULDN'T have been more proud when Shayna told me she was investing in herself and getting some coaching. We met when her nagging discomfort was she thought the world, including her husband, did not have confidence in her abilities. As a result, neither did she. Shayna had owned a previous business where she made several costly mistakes after giving it her blood, sweat and tears. She was letting those experiences influence her self-worth in the present. As you can imagine, the words she used to describe herself were far from empowering.

For Shayna, one of the most important tools she adopted was the phrase, "In the past I…but now I…" With it, she learned to not just leave the past in the past, but also learn from those mistakes to make better decisions in the present. We also focused on awareness and catching herself when the disempowering words flowed more out of habit than truth. However, instead of punishing herself for her conditioned response, she began to rewire it. She began to separate emotions from her identity. She was no longer a failure; she was a work in progress. She even had the courage to reflect back to her old business and make a list of what she did well so she could bring those qualities into her current one. Slowly, Shayna began to change not just the words she used to describe herself, but the actions she took from an empowered place. Today, Shayna stands a little taller when talking about her growth, her business and herself. Not only that, but as she began to change how she spoke to herself, so did the people around her thus creating a positive self-talk loop. As for her business, it's popping. She recently wrote me that she had the biggest sales month...Of her life!

5.

THE POWER OF BELIEFS

STORIES YOU ACCEPT AS TRUTH

As we saw before, beliefs are a series of thoughts, or a story you repeat so often you are sure it is correct. Hence, the difference between a belief and a mere thought is that a belief is something that you have deeply internalized as *truth*. As such, beliefs wield an enormous influence in your life, and is your third superpower. They are the gatekeepers of your internal world which dictate what actions you will take in your external one.

We know that in order for you to grow you need to have 20% of discomfort which becomes the driving force for your internal change. Where many personal development books fall short, in my opinion, is that they give you tools but they don't work with the underlying beliefs that make those tools powerful. You can temporarily change the way someone thinks about something, but if their belief system is not aligned, that change won't last. It's why so many New Year Resolutions fail. You want to lose weight, but your belief system doesn't support that change. Deep down, you think it will be difficult or maybe that you are not worthy of a healthy body. Same is true as you read this book. If you are just nodding along with me as you read, but inside you are not really internalizing your superpowers, then the change I am promising you will not happen. Alignment is the only way to ensure success with anything. I have done a million things in my life, I have been both successful and unsuccessful at them: businesses, relationships, parenting, etc. I have found that when I am not in alignment with what I am doing, when my beliefs are not compatible with the actions I need to take, there is no way I will succeed. That is why a little later we will dive into actions. Still, I wanted to introduce the topic of alignment here so that as you work on your beliefs, you choose those that are both empowering *and* feel good to you. Otherwise, the rest doesn't matter.

....

Beliefs are the gatekeepers of your internal world dictating which actions to take in your external one.

....

BELIEFS DETERMINE if, or which, actions you will or will not take. Sure, you can power through doing things you don't believe in, but eventually you will experience burnout and be right back at the drawing board. With effort, beliefs can be changed to empower and better serve you. Let's take a deeper look at them.

THE REAL TRUTH ABOUT BELIEFS

You ACQUIRE beliefs both consciously and unconsciously. Some are based on facts, like mathematical principles: 2+2 = 4. Others are based on experience; you have witnessed something multiple times and your personal experience caused you to believe that is true. Or finally, you gain beliefs because they were passed to you by your family of origin. Your parents passed on to you what they were taught to believe from their parents, who were taught to believe that from their parents and so on. And if not your parents, then your teachers, mentors, society, and your environment. Sometimes, deeply held beliefs are not based on facts. Actually, some of our most powerful beliefs are based on faith and cultural norms. If whoever raised you was, for example, a Christian, then chances are you would have Christian beliefs yourself. If, however, you were born in India and your parents were Hindi you probably would hold that belief system instead of the Christian one.

Humanity has fought wars based on beliefs. Not just on religion but on morals of what is right and wrong. Nazis believed Jews were inferior and launched an extermination campaign against them. Polygamists believe it is beneficial to society to have multiple wives. Atheists believe there is no God. You have a set of beliefs too. You might believe that you are not good at math, or that you are not good enough.

Or you may believe that anything is possible and that you are a great dancer. You may not even realize how deep these are, and how much influence they wield in your life. I have no idea about your current beliefs, but I do know that paying attention to them, though perhaps challenging, can be one of those levers you pull which causes everything to change. I'm not here to change your religious beliefs, or any belief, really. I want you to understand them so that you are empowered to look at them and decide for yourself whether the beliefs you are holding onto are serving you or not. Let's use the example of money. This could be a scenario:

> Thought: *It is hard to make money.*
> Belief: *If I want to be rich, it will be very hard.*

YOU HOLD this belief as truth because growing up you saw your parents struggling to make ends meet or to give you the little extra luxuries you wish you had. They were tired at the end of the day, and sometimes when you asked for something they looked at you in disbelief: "How could you be asking for that? Don't you see how hard it is to pay the bills?" If your belief is that it's hard to make money, then getting rich and breaking that cycle, the story goes, will be incredibly hard to do. And so, you hop on the struggle bus.

> Actions: You don't start a business because you are not rich, and it will be hard to make money from it. You get a job instead.
> Results: You continue to struggle with money because you are caught in a job that doesn't pay you nearly

enough for the effort you put in. You pass on the belief that money is hard to make to your children.

Now, HERE is another scenario. When I was younger, I had huge self-esteem issues and felt unworthy of love.

Thoughts: I have no positive qualities, no one will ever love me.
Belief: I am doomed to a life of loneliness.
Action: If someone pays even the least attention to me, I cling on to them as if my life depended on it.
Results: My relationships eventually failed because I was so needy, just perpetuating the belief that no one will ever love me.

Now, LET's look at how a belief can positively influence you.

Thought: I can do anything because though hard, it will be possible.
Belief: Nothing is impossible (hint, hint).
Actions: Take a chance and start a business / ask someone on a date / cross the Atlantic on a rowboat.
Results: Be a wildly successful entrepreneur / find a soul mate / be Instagram famous.

BELIEFS GO both ways. They can help or hinder you. They can keep you stuck in the stories of generations past, or they can help you break paradigms and elevate your experience. Beliefs dictate who shows up to the party: an empowered you or a shackled you. Beliefs drive you. They are your catalyst, so it is important to pay attention to them.

Contrary to some organized systems, we should encourage the challenging of beliefs. As a philosophy major, I was taught to form arguments. For every paper I wrote, and there were many, I had to state my premise and then list three objections someone could have about my premise. I mentioned earlier that I anticipated your reservations about the 20% Power Principle of Discomfort and tried to address them as I described it to you. I have tried to do that as you have progressed through this book with sample objections.

....

Doubt brings change or it brings certainty.
Doubt everything.

....

NEW BELIEFS come from questioning our inherited ones. We will either reinforce them and believe at a deeper level or change them to more empowering ones. If I got sober, gained self-esteem, and entered into an empowered relationship with Joe, I didn't have to be needy and therefore our relationship lasted until death did us part.

The strongest beliefs, in my opinion, come from your experiences. It's why EmpowerFit is all based on physically active games. Because you experienced that story in your body, it becomes even more embedded and real. In the case of the children yelling out their power words, they are experiencing the word "brave" or "powerful" as they struggle to continue the game. They are also saying it, hearing it, listening to others say they're words. That creates a much more powerful experience.

Here's another example: I hold the belief of the 20% Power Principle of Discomfort. No one taught it to me, but after sitting with that story, observing over and over again how people I coach redefine what is possible for themselves when they embrace this and seemingly do the impossible, this principle became a cemented belief. I have enough evidence to trust in it, and I constantly re-affirm it as I observe and notice it in action as I lead my daily life.

Beliefs can be internal or external in their focus. You can have a belief about society, religion, politics, what other people do. Those are outwardly focused. But some beliefs are internal, about yourself. They inform your identity and the words you use to describe yourself.

Now, this is going to sting a bit, but stay with me. We all hold disempowering beliefs, here and there. And we hold on to them tightly because there is a secondary payoff to us.

If my belief is that I am not good at math, then I can hide behind that and not challenge myself by doing the accounting for my business. I need to hire a bookkeeper because you know, I'm not that great at math and don't want to make a mistake.

Or, if my belief is that it is unsafe to drive at night, then I can pass that on to my kids and they may not drive at night as often as they would otherwise because they too believe that it's not safe. Holding on to that belief, serves me in manipulating my children. Positive beliefs also have a payoff, and as you can imagine, a much more empowering one. One such belief that I hold is that nothing is impossible. Let me explain.

 # NOTHING IS IMPOSSIBLE

BELIEVING THAT nothing is impossible gives you the courage and resolve to tackle what is in your 20% of discomfort. The only caveat with this belief in particular is that yes, anything is possible as long as it doesn't go against the laws of nature. So, for example, you can't be born an adult and die a baby. But for everything else? Then it's just a matter of figuring it out.

I cannot understate the importance this belief has had in my life. So much so that it is a critical part of the EmpowerFit curriculum I teach children. And if you can believe that, then everything is "figureout-able," as Marie Forleo says. Then that 20% of discomfort you are facing is no longer a showstopper—every new challenge becomes a new character in the story that takes the plot to the next level.

In our curriculum we have children play a game where one partner has to try to find something impossible, and the other child has to find a solution. If someone thinks they found something impossible, then they bring it to the whole group. Together, they need to find a way for it to be possible. By the end of the exercise, the belief that nothing is impossible is prevalent within the group and it's a great base for which to continue teaching the curriculum and for encouraging children through struggle as they now believe that anything is possible. But it takes a little work to really hold on to this belief, so let's go through some examples. In my work, any time I ask a group of children "What's impossible?" at least one will shout out: "It's impossible to fly!" Conversations usually go something like this:

ME: "Well, have you ever been in an airplane? That is flying!"

CHILD: "That is not what I meant. I meant a person!"

ME: "Well, have you ever seen a wingsuit? Those people are flying. Or a ski jumper in the Olympics, they are flying. A person jumping off a plane with a parachute, isn't that person flying? A person can fly, but maybe not like a bird. It's with the assistance. 'Flying' may not end up meaning what you first envisioned, but it can happen in a different way."

CHILD: "But I meant it is impossible for me to pick up my feet and begin to fly."

ME: "Well, true. It is impossible right now to pick up your feet, flap your arms, and begin to fly...not yet! But technology is changing every day. Today we have drones and hoverboards so, if what you really want, above all else, is to pick up your feet and fly, chances are you will be able to in the future. You can't do that yet, but I am certain that you could get there. Maybe *you* will be the person to invent a way to do it!"

SOMETIMES, A more concrete example might help. For example, you might wonder, can a quadriplegic woman be a triathlete? Sure, she can! Just ask my friend Kerry with whom I raced several races including a triathlon. She cannot move her body, so if you imagine her competing in the traditional way, then she can't compete. However, she is an adaptive athlete. With the help of equipment and volunteers, there are numerous adaptive athletes who participate in all sorts of endurance events ranging from 5Ks to marathons, triathlons, and mud runs. They may not look like other athletes, but *they are* competing!

And, though controversial I will say this: anything that can be fixed with money is not a real problem. The real problem is that you don't have that money, and you can probably fix that. For example, let's say that you want to be a doctor and the price of college is absurd. The problem is not that you can't be a doctor, the problem is that you may not have the money to go to school to become that doctor. Health on the other hand, now *that's* a real problem. No money in the world could've saved Joe's life. For everything else, there's Mastercard. Just kidding, that a reference to a popular commercial in the nineties. But for everything else that can be fixed with money, there is a solution. You just need to find it.

Pretend you want to sit in a chair and there is no chair around you. The chair is not the problem—it exists, you just need to find it. Maybe you are in a town where there are no chairs at all. *Anywhere.* That is still not a problem because the chair exists, you just need to find it. Maybe you go to the next town over, or maybe you go to the forest, chop a tree, and make a chair. But the chair? The solution for your desire to sit on a chair exists.

But we don't live life that way.

We worry about the things that aren't real problems. Generally, we have two flavors of worry. One is that we won't get what we want, while the other is that once we do get it, we will lose it. The fear of not getting what we want is a driver: it leads us to try new things and pushes us forward because we want that thing whether that is money, a new relationship, a good grade, or a new skill.

The second keeps us stuck. You made it, you have the money, relationship, promotion whatever, but now you are afraid it won't last, or you will lose it. You worry someone might steal it, the economy will crash, or that you will somehow mess things up. You become averse to risk and focused on protecting versus growing.

WHEN THINGS aren't going well, we think there is no solution. But there is.

We may not *like* the solution. But that doesn't mean it doesn't exist. Perhaps the solution is bankruptcy, or the solution is a divorce. Neither of those things are pleasant. But on the other side of it, there will be something new.

....

Many things may seem impossible,
but in reality, they are not. They are just difficult.

....

CHALLENGES AREN'T insurmountable obstacles. View them rather as problems to be solved or, even better, as questions in search of answers. Too often we use the word "impossible" as an excuse for giving up. We always have a choice. The game is not over until *you* stop playing it or your body doesn't keep up with it.

But most of us quit too early. And quitting can look different depending on the situation. Oftentimes, quitting means stopping. I quit a twelve-hour bike race at hour eight because I was mentally beaten. But at other times quitting means inaction, not looking for a solution. Perhaps someone in a toxic relationship doesn't leave that relationship because they are afraid of being alone and starting over. That's quitting too. Either way, we stop searching for the change and we just say it's impossible. But what would happen if you lived in the world of possibility? What would happen if you embraced "Nothing is Impossible"? What would you be willing to do, and what would you be willing to risk? It's a loaded question. But it's essential. Whatever you are facing might suck a this very moment, but it will pass and give way to something different. This is the heart of the 20% Power Principle. Because nothing is impossible, it is up to you to rise to the challenge and own the discomfort so that you can evolve and grow your container.

HOW TO UPLEVEL YOUR BELIEF SYSTEM TO SUPPORT YOUR GROWTH

Now that you are familiar with beliefs, how do you work with yours? How do you decide which ones are constructive and which ones are holding you back? And how do you build empowering ones instead? My favorite part is teaching you tools that will change your life, and I promise you these tools, if applied, will.

Because our belief system often comes from our cultural conditioning, that is, what we were taught from our environment, sometimes it's hard to understand why we have them. This is why it's useful to deconstruct the beliefs and get to the bottom of why you think the way you think. You'll ultimately see what made that belief true for you.

Deconstructing Beliefs: The 7 Whys

This is a very powerful exercise that brings enormous clarity, if you are open and honest with yourself. Take one belief that seems central to the others. Let's use health as an example. Perhaps your belief is that it's hard to be healthy. This is disempowering and will make it less likely for you to go out of your way to make healthier choices.

Belief: It is hard to be healthy.

Now ask yourself: Why is that?

"Because unhealthy options are easier to prepare."

Why?

"Because I buy prepackaged foods in the supermarket."

Why?

"Because I don't have time to make a healthy meal from scratch."

Why?

"Because I am busy doing all the things for everyone in this house."

Why?

"Because I am the mom and no one else will do it."

Why?

"Because I don't ask for help."

Why?

"Because I don't trust anyone with my kids."

Why?

"Because I had a traumatic childhood, and I don't want my kids to have one too."

BINGO. Now you are unpacking the belief that it is hard to be healthy. And though all those things are valid, the real issue to work on is, "I had a traumatic childhood and don't want my kids to have one too." Because of this, you don't trust anyone and feel you have to do it all yourself, and since you are human some things fall through the cracks, and buying prepackaged foods is a time- and life-saver.

There is nothing wrong with buying prepackaged foods. But if you do this exercise and you see "I'm buying prepackaged foods because I don't have time to cook because I can't do everything and I don't trust anyone to take care of my kids," You can then *own* that and see what part of this belief cycle you want to change to address the discomfort of not being as healthy as you'd like to be.

I am not discarding your traumatic childhood experience that led to all of this. If this were a new discovery, a lot of feelings might have been stirred up. Take the time to process them by journaling or seek professional help if this is something you haven't explored before. Sure, it sucks to revisit old wounds that haven't healed properly, but now you know exactly what is holding you back. Why keep picking at a scab if you can let it heal and show off a badass scar?

If you have already worked on those issues and can see

them as just part of your story but not who you are today, then continue accepting them. The trauma stays in your past; it can inform your present, but only you get to choose what impact they have on your future. Like you, I've had plenty of bad things happen, but from where I stand, those things are my history. They made me who I am today, but the past only affects me to the extent I let it. For example, writing my story of being in a mental institution was by no means a pleasant experience. As I mentioned before, I almost didn't share it with you. But I am not the same person who was sitting on that couch. Therefore, I can look at her with love and compassion, understanding it was a different point in my life. It informs my present, but it by no means holds me back from my future. Again, I am not encouraging toxic positivity here. I am encouraging acceptance and empowering you to acknowledge the past. I am also encouraging you to decide *today* how much or how little of it you want to continue living in.

There is a loop theory where the past creates the beliefs that lead you to the present. The present is where you take actions that influence your future. That future will eventually be your present. The cycle continues on and on for the rest of your life until you decide to break it by changing your beliefs, and by tackling your 20% discomfort where all of that stuff lives.

Here's an example. When I was in college, I was carjacked. It was the summer of 1993, my parents lived in Miami, and I had gone home for an internship. I worked at Goodwill Industries which was located in Liberty City. At the time, Miami was violent, and Liberty City was at the center of it. I knew that when I took the job, but I spent a lot of my younger years working in slums and disenfranchised communities in the United States and abroad.

I was going to work late that day. It was around 11:00 a.m. and John Secada was playing on the radio. I was driving my mom's red Honda Accord with the window open since I was smoking a cigarette, and she didn't know I smoked. Here I was singing and daydreaming at the red light when I saw a kid walk towards my car while scanning his head from side-to-side.

Hmmm, I thought, *that's odd*. I threw the cigarette out and began to roll up the window because something about that kid made me uncomfortable. Before the window was fully up, he was at my door with a gun to my head. I did what I always do when I get scared: I froze. Eventually, I got out of the car, and he hopped in and drove away with it. He was found five hours later, and I had the car back that same afternoon. Still, having a gun to my head was rather traumatic.

Ten years later, in my early thirties, I moved to Miami. By then I had already lived in New York, California, and Santiago de Chile. I worked at a homeless shelter in downtown which at the time, was also a violent neighborhood. And guess what would happen? As soon as I took the highway exit to downtown, I would freeze. My anxiety would skyrocket as I drove through the side streets and to the relative safety of the shelter. My past experience influenced how I perceived the present. It also influenced the future.

Once I am aware of my beliefs, stories, and patterns then I can see how this trauma infiltrates my life. From that empowered perspective I can deliberately *choose* to accept the past and change those beliefs so that I can have a different future that doesn't keep circling back to the same trauma over and over again.

You don't have to fix everything all at once. Maybe you realize you are not willing to work on your trust issues right now, but you are on time management. Cool, do that. Perhaps you realize there are some people you could trust with your kids after all, and you can ask them for help to give you time to go to the gym. Cool, do that.

Unpacking your beliefs is going to give you a road map to help change and confront the discomfort that is currently in your 20%. Based on that, you can develop strategies that will better serve you instead of keeping you stuck in this loop.

"But how do you build more empowering beliefs?"

I'M NOT a big fan of repeating affirmations over and over again hoping that something changes. When I first started doing affirmations, I felt like a fraud. I was telling myself one thing and feeling something completely different. And though I still do my affirmations, and I teach a special way of doing it to my clients, the Belief Table is an even better and more powerful tool. I learned this when I was first starting my business and had no sales experience. I felt like an imposter: "Who is going to listen to me?" And I didn't think anyone would ever pay even a dime to get my help. My sales coach had me create Belief Tables, and so my love for this tool began.

 **THE BELIEF TABLE**

IMAGINE ONE of those bar tables that have one leg to support the tabletop. They are cute and efficient when it comes to space management, but they are rather unbalanced because they only have one source of support. Now imagine a dining room table. That one usually has four legs to support the tabletop. That dining room table is much sturdier than the bar one. But what if a table had fifty legs supporting it? Other than the fact that you probably wouldn't be able to sit and put your legs underneath it, that table and tabletop, they're firm and not going anywhere.

The same thing happens with a belief. Let's say you want to believe you are someone who finishes what you start. But when you say that to yourself, you kind of vomit a little because deep down, you don't think it's true. You can repeat to yourself "I am someone who finishes what I start," till the cows come home, but you still won't believe it. You need to find *evidence*. You need to prove to yourself that you are indeed someone who finishes what you start. Chances are you really do, but you don't notice those things. We usually notice the things we *didn't* do, instead of all the things we have accomplished. Negative bias and all.

Therefore, the belief, "I am someone who finishes what I start" is the tabletop. We now need to give it legs — fifty to be exact. Underneath the tabletop, you will write fifty examples of why that belief is true. The first thirty or so pieces of evidence might be easy. I promise you there will come a point where you are not at fifty, and you will say, "I don't have fifty, this is not true." That is your belief limit: the point from which you can't see further. However, your discomfort is right beyond that point, so push yourself and get to fifty. This will require you to go deeper and remember things that maybe you had forgotten. That is where the magic lives.

"But Cristina, you don't understand.
I don't have fifty things that I have finished."

YOU DO. It's just you are probably thinking of only the big things. Maybe you haven't finished writing a book, or you haven't finished decorating your room, or building your team. That's okay, but did you eat today? If so, you started a meal and you finished it. Did you go somewhere? If so, you started a trip and finished it. Did you wash your hands? If so, you started washing your hands and you finished. You already are someone who starts and finishes; you just don't focus on the stuff that you accomplish.

"That's a cop out, Cristina. I mean in the big things."

GUESS WHAT my friend? How you are in the little things is how you are in the big things. Maybe you haven't completed a major project *yet*, but you have probably taken a lot of smaller actions which combined will lead you to complete that task. Why not celebrate that? Why deny yourself the belief that will empower to change something? I mean, as that same coach would tell me, "You are welcome to argue for your limitations as much as you'd like." But nothing productive will come out of it. However, if you do your Belief Table as I am showing you here, I guarantee you that in the end, you will feel better than when you started. You will remember big things in the past that you completed but didn't acknowledge.

"Okay, but what if I want to be a famous soccer player and I am nowhere near that?"

WELL, IN that case your belief wouldn't be "I am a famous soccer player." You need to have a belief that you can grab on to. For example: I am strong/willing/able enough to become a famous soccer player. And from *that* point, write your Belief Table. I have not made the team before, but I will continue playing. I work out every day to get stronger. I have made my way out of the bench, etc., etc., until you have fifty pieces of evidence as to why you are strong/willing/able enough to become a great soccer player.

Once you have your list, read it. Anytime you begin to doubt yourself just go back and read it so you can prove to yourself (again) that you have what it takes, and that belief is true. When you are changing something so deeply rooted in yourself it's not going to be a one and done thing. New layers of doubt will show up, and when they do, just read your list again, add to it or even create a whole new one. *You* are in control of your thoughts. Beliefs are just thoughts you have internalized as truth. You get to choose whether you use a Belief Table to construct new and empowering beliefs that will help you reach your goals...or not.

This exercise is SO powerful I cannot encourage you to do it enough. I even used all caps here; that's how much I believe in this tool! Do it anytime you hit a rough patch, anytime you want to change something about yourself, anytime you need to construct a new belief that will empower you to move through your discomfort.

To get you started, let me share with you some of the many Belief Tables I have done to empower myself to move forward in my 20% discomfort. In past years, these have been related to my business and feeling like I could build it.

> I can be a successful entrepreneur.
> My clients' lives are better after working with me.
> I am able to build a business without sacrificing my family.
> I can support my family as a single widowed mom.
> My message is important enough to write a book (wink wink).

An important thing to remember when trying to change your beliefs is that they need to be in alignment with who you are at the present moment. You will change and grow, so the future you might be able to grab onto the belief that you can be a Fortune 500 CEO if that is your goal. But the present you is struggling to pay rent. That is a big gap.

And while I am all for envisioning and imagining a future that includes all the things I want but don't have right now, and that is a fun exercise that lifts my spirits, a Belief Table is different. You are convincing yourself of something that is attainable by providing evidence that you are already on the path there.

The 20% Power Principle of Discomfort is itself a belief. As I told you earlier, I came to this belief from my own personal experience, and it became so powerful to me that I wanted to share it with the world.

Remember, this belief has two parts: first, that everyone has 20% discomfort and second, that this is a good thing because it causes us to take action and grow. The entire purpose of this book is to empower you with this belief. But ultimately, *you* get to decide whether to adopt it or not. And you will decide based on whether this belief supports whatever thoughts you have expressed as words.

Molly's Story

MOLLY WANTED a change in her life: she was tired of feeling second fiddle to her husband. She loved him very much and divorce was never on her radar, she just didn't like who she was becoming. She had wanted to stay home when her kids were born, and her husband was the sole provider. Overtime, Molly felt she couldn't make even basic decisions on her own. She felt she needed to ask permission to buy anything even if her husband never asked that of her. She felt constrained and would never really go "all in" leading her to unconsciously self-sabotage. This also showed up in her business. She invested in coaching but then wouldn't pay the fees to register her company or pay the dues for her website. Something always came up and Molly would find a way to stop her progress. After a few cycles of this pattern, she finally decided to dig into her cultural conditioning to understand what was going on.

WITH AN open mind, Molly used the "7 Whys" tool and was able to connect her cultural conditioning to her self-sabotage. She came from an abusive background where her stepfather would get angry if she spent any of "his" money. And though her husband was very caring and kind, she couldn't break the belief that he would resent her if she spent "his" money too. Bingo. We were working on the wrong thing. Molly didn't really want to start the business she hired me to help her with, she wanted to not feel like she was a kid again depending on someone else. She didn't need to start a business to do that, she needed to create a new belief that she was worthy to have the things she needed, even if she wasn't the one who made the money to pay for them.

HOW TO COMPARE WITHOUT DESPAIR

WHILE TALKING about beliefs, let's take a sidestep and talk about one thing we do to ourselves, that constantly hurts us, and that we are usually not aware of. Let's talk about the silly comparison game we all play. Maybe by understanding it, you can break the thought pattern and create an empowering one instead. When we compare ourselves to others, more often than not, we lose.

There will always be someone "more" than you; someone will be richer, thinner, or more successful. We are one amongst many. Let's review the three main destructive ways in which we compare ourselves to others, because I can guarantee you have fallen victim to these at one point or another. Let's end this compare and despair pattern once and for all.

Comparing One to Many

THE FIRST type of comparison we make is compare all of who we are, to one aspect of someone else. Let's pretend you have a friend, John. He is wicked smart. He was called by NASA to figure out an issue with the International Space Station. And here you are: I mean, you can barely compute a 15% tip in your head. Oh, and then there's your friend Jane; she is so healthy and fit that she won her age group at the Boston Marathon. Not only that, but she only has 2% body fat, and she's so strong that she can lift a car with her pinky. And here you are: you're lucky if you can chase your kids around the park. And Delisa? Well, Delisa is Mom of the Year. She's PTA President, her kids are always dressed impeccably, and they love vegetables. Any time the teacher needs something, Delisa is there to help. And here you are: you just forgot to send the cupcakes to school. Thankfully, Delisa swooped in and took care of it. And then there is Jason, and Julie, and on, and on you go noticing how everyone around you is better than you. What you didn't consider is that you are comparing one quality someone has to all of who you are.

This is not about putting someone down to make yourself feel better, but it is about not selling yourself short. Maybe you play tennis better than John. Mary can't cook to save her life, and Delisa is so uptight that she has no friends. Yes, these people are extraordinary in one field, but you never know what the rest of their lives look like. Even the best in the world at something, has their 20% of discomfort they need to work on. But you probably never looked at the whole person.

Comparing all of your faults—and we all have our faults—to the *top* quality that someone else has is just being unfair to yourself. All you accomplish is that you feel "less than" and disempowered. What if, instead, you changed that story and admired each person for their particular talents while recognizing you have yours too? If you don't believe you have at least one single solitary talent to share with the world, I think you need to look in the mirror and challenge that thought, because I guarantee you have way more than one.

Comparing Insides to Outsides

THE SECOND negative comparison we make is between someone else's *outside* and your *inside*. Take Delisa the supermom. She's always smiling and available for her children's teacher. But inside, she just wishes she could be funny because her kids never laugh with her. She's too busy making sure they look impeccable. Maybe these struggles are causing a rift in her marriage and she's about to get a divorce. Or maybe John is super-lonely because he can't find anyone outside of work with similar interests, and maybe runner Jane wanted to go pro but never had the guts to do so and lives a life full of regret.

We're all fighting a private battle others know nothing about. You see neither the battles nor the internal scars. Still, when you compare your inside to their outside, you're bound to lose every time. What you see on social media is not reality, it's a manicured life someone carefully shows you; it's an image that someone wants you to believe represents them. It's their outside, don't measure against your inside.

Comparing Your Chapter One to Their Chapter Ten

PERHAPS YOU just started learning how to play the guitar, and you see your friend Matt over there, picking as if his fingers had independent brains. They go so fast. You look at Matt and think, *"Wow, look at what Matt can do. I really suck at playing guitar."* But you have been playing for a few weeks, while Matt has been playing for a few decades. Experience is a continuum; Matt is simply further along in that continuum. He's had more time to practice, that is all.

I get this a lot working with clients, and I can tell you with 100% certainty that I can teach you these tools *not* because I'm special or have some God-given talent, but because I have been working them for a long time. When you look at mentors, or people who have more knowledge and skill, don't compare yourself to them. Chances are you're barely starting the journey they have been on for years. It's like a baby who's learning to crawl feeling bad because her sister can run without falling over. Nonsense. Instead of feeling "less than" because you are just starting your Chapter 1, look at the person in their Chapter 10 as *inspiration* not intimidation. What can you learn from them and their journey? What would you do differently if you were them? Can they teach or mentor you? Learn from them. Don't compare yourself to someone further along. Once again, you will lose every time.

HOWEVER, WE cannot improve what we don't measure. Who do we compare ourselves with to measure our progress? The only person you should compare yourself with is with who you were yesterday. No one in this world is like you. To quote Dr. Seuss, there is no one you-er than you. Comparing yourself to someone else will always be as if you are comparing apples to oranges. But when you compare yourself to who you were yesterday, last month, or last year, that is a fair—apples to apples—measurement of progress. Are you making steady advances towards your goals? Are you moving in the direction you want to? That is the only thing that counts.

Here is a great exercise to do if you are struggling with a relationship where you are a little jealous of someone. Journal about what you are feeling and ask yourself what you are comparing about that person that is making you feel small. There is a very good chance you will find that you are falling into one of these three 'compare and despair' patterns.

What about competing with others?

I AM a big fan of competition. And again, just as the only person with whom you should compare yourself should be yesterday's version of you, the same is true of competition. Your opponent is there to bring out the best in you. You already know that I didn't view myself as an athlete even as I was competing at an Ironman triathlon. But there's more to it. When I first started training for triathlons, before I even signed up for Ironman, I was part of a training team.

WEDNESDAY MORNINGS, 5:45 a.m. was track practice. Every so often, the coach would give us a speed test; a good thing to do to measure progress. The only problem was that I was the slowest person on the team, and he would post everyone's times on an Excel spreadsheet, from fastest—which was usually Joey—to slowest, which was usually me.

It was *mortifying* not only to see my name as the last one

of thirty runners, but also see the time difference between my time and Joey's. It was borderline ridiculous. And though Joey was a friend and eventually became my coach, and though we started the same races at the same time, I was not competing with Joey. But here is the deal: *Running with people who are faster than you makes you faster.*

Most Saturday mornings I rolled out of bed at an ungodly hour to meet up with this group of runners. We'd hit the sidewalks for anywhere between five and twenty-five miles. We'd start together, but in less than two minutes, I was alone. I couldn't keep up. Why was I killing myself to get there so early if I was running with someone for literally less than five minutes? But I kept showing up because those few minutes helped me get faster as I tried to stay with them for longer stretches of time.

The biggest gift is to find a competitor who is just a little above your skill level. I like long races because then I don't have to push my heartrate and go too fast. That's why marathons and Ironman competitions are appealing to me. I could walk to China if I had to, just don't ask me to get there fast. In long races, when some people start fading, I'm like the energizer bunny that keeps going. Therefore, a 10K (6.2 miles) is a horrible distance for someone like me. In it, you can't go too slow and outlast the faders, but you also can't go all-out as the distance requires some endurance. In other words, a nightmare.

Meanwhile, I befriended a woman we'll call Tammie who was just a little faster than me. Nothing like Joey; I could at least keep her in sight, if not stay at her side. One day, Tammy and I got in a tiff about something or other. I don't even remember what now, but at the time it seemed like a big deal, and I was pissed. When Tammy showed up to the same 10K race I did, my competitive side also showed up and I wanted to win. For all I knew she wasn't racing me, she probably couldn't care less, but in my head, I was racing *her*.

The gun went off, I began to run a little too fast for my pace, but I could spot her. When she slowed down to get water, I took advantage and passed her. Now you have to understand, that is not me. I am not a racer like that. I stop to drink water, talk to people, I'm a tourist racer. But that day, I ran faster than I ever have. I could see her behind me, and was determined to keep it that way. I still remember the feeling of the last half mile. I began to run faster and faster. My side hurt as if someone had shot me, and I was not breathing, but gasping for any air to get into my lungs. I thought I was going to die right then and there, but I didn't. I crossed the finish line in front of Tammy and in well under an hour.

I NEVER ran a 10K again!

That day I didn't race against Tammie. I raced against the one-hour mark. To run a 10K in under an hour for someone like me was a daunting goal because I knew it would hurt and be so ridiculously uncomfortable. So, if Tammie hadn't been at the same race, I may not have had the motivation to run so fast that I almost passed out. But because she was, and I did not want to lose to her, I ran faster than ever.

This is a lesson we teach the kids at EmpowerFit. You thank your competitors not just because it's the polite thing to do. You thank them because they push you to go beyond your current limitations. They push you to grow. We encourage competition. We turn everything into a race, so children experience winning and losing, and begin to look at their competitors as gifts to push them to reach their goals. What if adults believed the same?

6.

THE POWER OF ACTION

NOTHING CHANGES IF YOU
DO NOTHING TO CHANGE IT

OUR FOURTH superpower is Action. Unless you take decisive and committed actions to tackle your 20% of discomfort, nothing will change. It's where the rubber meets the road. You have already taken some actions, you are reading this book, you might have done some of the exercises to hone your other superpowers. Actions are often specific to the area of your life you are working on. If your discomfort comes from your job, the action might be to speak with your manager, ask for a raise, look for another job, work on your resume, etc. If your discomfort is in relationships, perhaps you will sign up for marriage counseling, plan for weekly date nights, or start a new hobby with your partner. Actions are specific to what you want to work on, however there are a few broad actions you can take that will help you regardless of what area of your life you focus on.

CHANGE STARTS WITH GIVING YOURSELF PERMISSION TO CHANGE

WHEREAS AWARENESS of your thoughts, words, and beliefs is a *mindset*, permission is the first *action* you must take in order to change. Yet, many of us don't give ourselves permission to be who we want to be, or even to own our discomfort. We allow our beliefs to exist unquestioned, whether they support us or not. And more, we need to give permission for others to own their 20% of discomfort. Allow them to handle it, it's not yours to deal with. In a way, I think it's simpler to allow other people to handle their 20% than it is for us to handle ours. Why? Because growth presents as a challenge, and challenges trigger our most primal instincts and pulls us into fear.

One of our basic human needs is for certainty, knowing what comes next and what we can count on. But as we saw earlier, certainty is an illusion. Control is an illusion. And when we are in our comfort zones, that illusion seems real. We feel safe.

Truth is, just as we have a need for safety and certainty, we also have a basic human need for variety. We get bored when life is plain and predictable all the time. We start searching for "excitement" in productive and unproductive places: a new a business, sport, or an illicit relationship. Simply put, after a while, our comfort zone begins to stifle us. That's when we start getting impatient with ourselves and with others.

Since Joe died, I have developed a rather irrational fear of running out of money. It's irrational because there is no amount of money in the bank that would make me feel safe, anyway. I could have ten million dollars and I probably would still feel that way because it is not *really* about the money, it's about making sure my boys have everything they need and, most importantly, that I could provide for them the same type of life they would've had if their dad was alive.

This fear rears its ugly head when my boys need something, and teenage boys need things constantly. My oldest outgrows his snowboard boots every season, the refrigerator is never fully stocked even if I go grocery shopping three times a week, and let's not start with college looming in the near future.

Fear. Fear that I won't have enough to do the things I want to do for them. Fear that I'm now a single mom and no longer a double-income family. Fear that I won't give them the opportunities they need to succeed in whatever they choose to do. When I am in fear, I do not behave well. I throw adult tantrums. I yell at my boys, and I become a helpless victim that the world is against. "If only you knew what I had to do and worry about, you'd pick up your darn room the first time I asked you to." Or "If only you knew the pressure I'm under, you wouldn't ask for this." It's unfair. It's unfair to them, and it's not my best self. Also, I am probably adding "fear of money" to the 20% discomfort they will have to deal with at some point. The first action I needed to take was to give myself permission to break the mold.

My INHERITED belief system told me happiness followed this path: school, college, work for a big name, get married, and have kids who would go to similar colleges, work in similar fields, and have similar marriages. Because that was the correct thing to do, it wasn't to be questioned. It was just right.

Much to my parents' chagrin, I deviated from that, often. They were catholic conservatives. I was a humanist hippy. But as much conviction as I had that I was living my life the way I wanted my life to be lived, underneath what seemed like my bold decisions was an immense amount of fear and insecurity. "What if I do life differently than what I was taught and then mess it up?" But more specifically:

"What if I parent differently, and then my kids suffer the consequences of my mistakes?"

I used to be riddled with fear and doubt and existential angst, really. Joe was my anchor. And together we created our own mold. We did things differently. We encouraged our boys to be musicians when it seemed that's what they were interested in. We went on four weeklong monumental road trips regardless of what sacrifices needed to be made to pull that off. We both were entrepreneurs who did *not* work for big name companies. We uprooted our family from Miami, Florida to Taos, New Mexico for no good reason other than give our boys a different experience. We were way off track of what both of our ancestors and parents would deem was "the right way to live."

Yet even if there was fear, I had an accomplice. I mentioned this before, that if I messed up our kids, Joe was part of the mess-up, and he could be blamed too. When in doubt, I could talk to Joe, and he would talk me off the ledge. Sure, we were living life differently, but we were doing it together.

And even with all that independence and rebellion, there were certain things we both wanted for our boys. There was a certain level of education, the ability to go on adventures around the world, the health to support these adventures, learn different languages, play lots of music, etc. All of these were part of our difference, and it cost money to create. We were working on that; we saved less and traveled more; shopped generic but experienced uniqueness.

Until there was no more together, and it was me alone.

Not only did I lose a funding stream to make these goals a reality, I also lost the person who shared them, the one who would tell me, "Don't worry, we will be okay." The same way our parents had expectations of how they would raise us, we had expectations of how to raise our children. We built a new mold, and now that mold was broken.

The mold included a life partner, a father, an income stream. The mold included stability, and the ability to give the boys all those experiences we wanted to. I was not going to be able to do this on my own.

This realization dawned on me at a boardercross snowboarding competition in Arizona, the same one Felipe lost in 2019.

I WAITED at the bottom of the hill. Joe hadn't been gone a month yet, and we were there...competing. I kept looking at the parents waiting for their children. When it wasn't their child coming down the mountain, they would talk to each other. They were doing things parents on the sidelines of children's sports do. I felt miserably alone; I didn't have my friends there nor did I have Joe. It was just me wondering if my boys would be okay. Wondering if coming all the way there to do this race so soon after their father's death was a good idea. Debating if they were strong enough, or if their head was in the right space, to handle a boardercross race.

I couldn't bounce my fears off anyone. No one was there to talk me off the ledge. I went deeper into doubt as I stood there waiting for my kids' turn. *What if I can't afford to send them to college? What if I can't take them on trips? What if, what if, what if…?* BOOM, an enormous wave of grief swept over me, and I had to go lick my wounds elsewhere as I burst into uncontrollable tears.

My kids were going to feel pain. Well, they already felt the loss of their dad, but they were also going to feel the loss of the life we had planned for them. I wanted desperately to keep things as close as possible to our life with Joe in it. In my mind, that life was the only way to lead them to happiness, and I was worried I wouldn't be able to provide it for them financially or emotionally.

But I was wrong. On the other side of that wave of grief and despair was another realization. If I can't provide for the mold Joe and I built for our family, it was up to me to build a new mold. One that I could shape, and which could provide for my boys what I thought was most important.

Even if I tried to go back to the mold my parents had, I couldn't. I was too far past it. I couldn't continue on the path that Joe and I were creating for our family either; that required Joe to be a part of it. I had the choice right then and there to see this as a curse or as an opportunity to re-create the belief system that I would pass on to my children. I chose the latter.

LETTING GO of expectations and creating life based on accepting where you are at is very difficult. It invites both doubt and loneliness. I have no one to share that burden with. But at the same time, once I accepted that life for my boys is going to be necessarily different, I stopped judging it as better or worse than what we had planned. It was pointless, and I didn't want to live the rest of our lives measuring what I was able to create for our family against a mold that requires two parents. If I did, I would come short every single time and it would keep me in a perpetual, disempowering loop.

Accepting my 20% of discomfort that life as I knew it, as I had wanted it to be, was over, accepting the mold was broken, gave me the opportunity to start building a new one where what matters is *internal* not external. That the amount saved, or the stamps on our passports are only as valuable as we allow them to be. The 20% Power Principle of Discomfort is essential because you don't get everything you want in life. But it's the quest for your dreams which makes life worth living. It's showing my boys how I struggle, but I eventually overcome. That things can get really hard, and weird, and yet we stick together. It's showing my kids that bad things happen even to good people, but it is up to us to continue being good. Showing that sometimes the 20% really sucks and it feels like you are 90% in the hole, but you are not. You can always grow your container.

I gave myself permission to think differently, to create new beliefs, and take new actions. One of those is writing this book that you are reading. And therefore, the results of these new actions will be different than the life I expected, but it will bring with it a joy of its own.

Yet sometimes we don't give ourselves permission to change and tackle the 20% of discomfort life throws at us. I see this a lot in women who want to start a business, or invest in coaching, but then back out in fear. They believe that investing in themselves means they are taking something away from their children.

When you don't give yourself permission to care for your 20% of discomfort you will resent other people who do set boundaries and work on theirs.

SOMETIMES, IN the case of these women who didn't dive into their discomfort to start their businesses, they try to control their child. Even if you are not a mom, see how you could be taking your lack of permission out on someone else.

The more you turn your back on your own desires and longings, the more you will resent the things that stop you from living in your purpose. And often, those "things" are actually the people you love the most, your kids and partner. Now, you don't necessarily do it intentionally, but if you reflect on it, you might see this pattern.

You're scrolling through Facebook, and you see a mom who gives herself permission to live the life she chooses, starting a business, playing tennis on Tuesday nights, or buying a dress. Whatever. You think something along the lines of *"Well sure, she can do that because she has a spouse who makes more money, or she doesn't have young kids, or <insert whatever judgmental reason you most like to use here>"* It stings a little because you feel you can't do that for yourself. Then your kid comes in asking you for something and, out of nowhere, you lash out: "No, you can't have that. You can't have everything you want."

Or perhaps you are driving to a job you don't like, stuck in traffic, and think, *"I can't quit because I need the money for my kid's braces."* Or *"I need to pay for the soccer travel team which costs a small fortune."* So, do you know what happens? And I am going to use a boy in this example. Well, that boy, he better be damn good at soccer, he better go to every practice without giving you grief, and he better play his best because you have sacrificed so much of your life for that kid to get a soccer scholarship to college. Even if he is still in elementary! You start controlling your child, who his friends are, what he does in his free time, what he eats, what he does at practice, what team he should play for, what birthday parties he attends. And if he decides he doesn't want to play soccer anymore? You demand of him, "Are you crazy? After everything I've done for you?"

Take a moment and let that sink in. I am the first one to raise my hand and admit these very words have come out of my mouth. Remember our chapter on words. It just wasn't about soccer; it feels terrible. I don't mean them, and my boys don't deserve it. More importantly, they're *not true*. All this turmoil comes from not giving yourself permission.

Therefore, let's bring this permission to break the mold into your life. Go back to your Life Inventory (Chapter 1), where you identified what is in your 20% of discomfort right now that you are willing to do something about. Ask yourself: "Have I given myself permission to change this?" "I am willing to do it sure, but do I allow myself to do *whatever I need to do* to change it?" "Do I feel like I will be hurting someone if I tackle this and if so, is that feeling valid, or does it hold me back?" "What resources (time, money, attention) will I need to tackle this discomfort?" And "Do I allow myself to be uncomfortable and invest these resources on myself?"

If you didn't answer *yes* to all of these, you have a permission issue. Maybe it's because you are a people pleaser, perhaps you are in a codependent relationship, or maybe you feel you don't deserve "it." I don't know. But I *do* know that nothing will change unless you give yourself permission to honor where you are and where you want to be.

So, how do you give yourself permission? It's super simple. Decide on what it is you want to give yourself permission to do, and then use the tools we already worked on. Be aware of your thoughts, question why you haven't given yourself permission before. Don't use disempowering words. Create a Belief Table around why you deserve to give yourself permission. You must have the belief that you are worthy of it otherwise you will never allow yourself to really tackle your 20% of discomfort and have whatever it is you desire.

 # GRATITUDE IS THE GOAT

WE TALK about gratitude, as *both* an action and a result. When you give yourself permission to work on your discomfort, you will feel gratitude for having the courage to change what is not working for you. But often, gratitude is an action. And it's not just any action, as I said, it is the GOAT of all actions. If you want to move from feeling down to feeling good, gratitude is the fastest (and easiest) way to get there. This is not just the woo-woo people who say this, neuroscientists have researched the chemical changes in the brain during states of gratitude and it literally affects your brain chemistry.

People often believe gratitude is what we do on Thanksgiving: I'm grateful for my house, and my family, yada, yada, yawn. Gratitude can be so much more than that; its effects are more lasting when you turn gratitude into a habit. So, let's look at three powerful gratitude practices that will help you navigate your discomfort with a little more ease.

Three Gratitude Practices to Instantly Shift Your Mood

MY ALARM clock is my dogs. They start whining and barking at precisely 6:30 a.m. to go on their walk. When my coaches suggest I meditate first thing in the morning, I explain, "I can't. Just no. I'm not willing to wake up even earlier. Plus, if my dogs sense I'm awake, they start barking and then what was the point of meditating while annoyed?" I had the same issue when my kids were little and would wake up before sunrise. I had to find a way to merge what I *had* to do with what I *wanted* to do. I could walk the dogs and meditate, but I like to close my eyes and that's difficult to do when walking. What I came up with was to use part of my walk to practice gratitude.

The first thing I do when I get out the door with the dogs is to list three things I am grateful for that morning. I don't commit to anything more than that because I don't want gratitude to be a chore, and three things are easy enough to do. What usually happens is that my list extends, I end up thinking about gratitude for about ten minutes! It is a wonderful way to start my day: by understanding that this day is a gift and whatever problems I will face between now and when I go to sleep are really nothing compared to the gifts I have. I don't just *say* I am grateful for my boys, and my dogs, and my house. I *feel* gratitude.

It sounds different. It's more like "I'm grateful that the air is cold, but the sun is out. It's the perfect weather and I am so happy I live in New Mexico and get to experience this almost every winter morning. I'm so grateful that my calendar is packed with calls and clients because I love coaching and creating new things and I *get* to provide for my family by doing something I love." I expand on the feeling of gratitude and by the end I am usually smiling, feeling like I am the luckiest person on earth, even if life is difficult sometimes, even if I am widow and single mom.

The morning of December 10, 2021 was the first day in our family history that started without Joe in it. I woke up, saw the boys asleep in our hotel room, and realized the nightmare was there when I had my eyes open, whenever I was awake. Sleeping was a reprieve. I remember it clearly: I went into the bathroom to not wake up the boys as I literally fell to my knees crying with a pain I had never experienced before.

After the wave of grief passed just enough for me to catch my breath, I lay on the bathroom floor and began my gratitude list. I knew that if I didn't, I would spiral down and I needed some connection to hope. It was the most powerful list of my life. I realized that even in my worst moment ever, there was still so much I could be grateful for. The boys were there with me, my sisters-in-law were coming to help me, my Facebook page was filled with messages of love and support, my house was being taken care of, my hotel bill was paid. I was in a daze. I was in crisis, but I felt loved and taken care of, and I couldn't have been any more grateful.

I was also grateful he died.

Granted, I didn't think that immediately. Joe might or might not have survived a little longer. If he made it out of the ICU, we would have had to live in Albuquerque at a rehab facility for months. He'd be on dialysis and probably chemo as they were not able to take all of his cancer out. He had always been very clear that if he could not go back to skiing, he did not want to get back at all. And that man was not going to be anywhere near a mountain. He might have lived a couple of months, maybe a little more. He would've been miserable, and he would've dragged the boys and I down with him. Not because he was mean, but because we loved him and would've been at his side with his misery and our own. In this ironic way, he gave us a gift. He cut the story short so neither of us would have to go through that torture. As hard as it is to be a widow, I will always remain grateful to Joe for being brave and deciding to be taken off life support. He was clear and determined, so I never had to question it. I share this with you because gratitude is something you can always reach for, even in your darkest moment, and it will immediately bring you comfort. It won't change anything about what is happening in the outside world, but it will give you the strength you need to face it.

THE SECOND gratitude tool I practice is one you might need tissues for, but it's wonderful, I promise. Get a picture of a person, either someone you love, or someone that you have to forgive, or a place, or an institution, but get a visual picture of something or someone. If this is your first time doing it, just get a picture of someone you love to make this easy. While looking at that picture and having that person in mind, tell them what you are grateful to them for. Let's say that you pick your sister, put a picture of her in front of you and begin to think, speak, or write. "Thank you, Lisa, for always being there for me, for the time you covered for me with Mom and Dad so I wouldn't get into trouble, for the dinner we had last night..." whatever comes to mind. That's all you have to do.

Gratitude doesn't have to be complicated to be powerful. Every time I do this, regardless of who I am doing it with, tears roll down my face. If they do for you too, welcome them because you're either releasing or appreciating something. That's what love feels like. This even happens when you do it with institutions! I did it looking at a picture of college, of the building of my first job on Wall Street, of the house I sold in Taos. It brought up all the good memories from those places. Enjoy it.

AND FINALLY, tool number three. I use this when I'm having a bad day, when people aren't doing what I need them to do, when the supermarket is out of my favorite chocolate, or I'm stuck in traffic. It takes less than three minutes, and you almost instantly shift your attitude. All you have to do is look around and start saying thank you to everything. Let's say that you're at the grocery store, and you're annoyed because they didn't have your favorite chocolate, but then you had to buy all kinds of other groceries, and you're stuck in line which is taking forever. If that's me, in my head I thank the cashier for being there doing her job even though she looks tired, and people are often mean. Thank you to the light at the register that lets me know they are open. Thank you to the credit card in my hand that allows me to pay for all this. Thank you to my family that gives me something to shop for, etc., and then when I've gone through the obvious ones, I look for others, however unlikely they might seem. Thank you to the cart that I'm pushing, because otherwise I wouldn't be able to carry everything. Thank you to the person who thought of putting my gum by the cash register because I might've forgotten to buy it and now, I can have it. Thank you to electricity, because the store can have lights so I can shop at night…And on, and on, and on, whatever you see, the next thing you see, you become grateful for that. Just do this for a couple of minutes. I don't know what it is about this practice that makes it so powerful, but I've never once felt worse when I finished than when I started. It instantly puts you in a better mood, and you forget that you were cranky to start with. It's a complete shift. I highly, *highly* recommend it.

Gratitude in action is so powerful because it changes how you feel. If you feel sad, angry, self-righteous (a personal favorite), etc., you focus on all the things going wrong. In gratitude you feel good and have access to more of the good parts of you: your creativity, imagination, hope...From that state, you get ideas and solutions because instead of "I can't believe I'm stuck in this line and the old lady in front of me is writing a freaking check, who does that?" you think, "Aww, isn't she cute, she still writes a check, who does that?"

My family, with whom I healed all relationships before my parents died, in Morocco in the late eighties. Don't mind the hair!

 # MAKE AMENDS TO FIND TRUE FREEDOM

Sometimes, it's hard to give ourselves permission when something from the past occupies a big part of our 20% of discomfort leaving little space for growth. Let's talk about cleaning our slate, sweeping our side of the street, and living with honor and integrity. The way to do that is by making amends.

I got this tool from going through the twelve steps of Alcoholics Anonymous. For all its faults and problems, I can honestly say AA saved my life. And in addition to finally taking responsibility, AA taught me that my actions have consequences, big and small. Sometimes you take a direct action, and it hurts someone. You blurt out something cruel in anger. Other times, your *inaction* is what's at fault. You didn't help a friend when they were sick and really needed you because you didn't feel like driving over. If you hammer nails into a piece of wood, you can take out the nails, but the holes are still there. There is still damage. Making amends is the equivalent of patching the holes. They won't be perfect, but they will be filled. If I wanted to stay sober, they told me, I would need to not just acknowledge what I did, but also make things right.

Believe me, it was the *last* thing I wanted to do. Going back to people I had hurt through my actions, face them, ask for forgiveness, and make it up to them was as enticing as a lobotomy. But doing so allowed me to move forward in life without the urge to run away from someone or something.

Everything you do, from where you buy your groceries to gossiping with your BFF affects people. Every action has a consequence and for that, my friend, you are responsible. The first part of making amends is to make a list of all the persons you have harmed. The litmus test here is easy. Let's say you're walking down the street and you spot someone from your past or present. If your instinct is to cringe and avoid them, they go on your list. If there's any reason why you wouldn't want to sit down and have coffee with them, unless it's because of something *they* did to *you*, that person also goes on your list.

If it's your friend Jane, who talks incessantly and you just don't feel like talking to her, obviously, it's different. Jane doesn't go on the list. But if you're hiding from Jane, because way back in middle school you kissed her boyfriend, she goes on your list even this happened 40 years ago. Be thorough, you have nothing to lose and everything to gain.

Note there is no blame, shame, or judgement here. I've done plenty of things I was not necessarily proud of, and you probably have as well. But the fact that you are willing to do something about it, to make it right, means you are no longer just the person who caused harm. You are now the person who also tried to make amends and take responsibility. This exercise will bring you a freedom you probably haven't experienced in a long time because we *all* have done things we aren't proud of, but most of us haven't made them right.

How do you know you did something wrong? I mean,

maybe they provoked you, or didn't they do it to you first? They might have acted wrongfully; they might have hurt you or caused you to react. That is on them, and if they were to do this exercise, you would be on *their* list. Think about it: what part did you play in the whole thing? Did you react inappropriately or disproportionately? In your reaction, did you cause harm? Don't think about what they did, think about *your* actions and yours only. You can't do anything about them, but you sure as heck can claim your power by cleaning your side of the street.

When it comes to our wrongs, they're usually divided into two types: there are *material* wrongs and *moral* wrongs. Material wrongs are actions that affect an individual in a tangible way; you borrowed money that you didn't pay back, or you were stingy, or you were using money to buy love. Other examples: you stole something, lied to someone, damaged property and didn't own it, fix it, or pay for it. Maybe that was a fender bender backing out of the parking lot or spray-painting a wall that wasn't yours. Perhaps it's that you buy your kid every gift under the sun because you feel you don't spend enough time with her. Or perhaps, you think the medical bill is disproportionally high, so you don't pay it.

Moral wrongs are inappropriate behaviors. For examples, setting a bad example for your child, being so consumed by your personal pursuits that you are unaware of the needs of others, lying to your boss to get out of trouble. Here would be things like sexual infidelity, broken promises, verbal abuse. We need to make amends for both material and moral wrongs.

Here's a hint: your parents and any siblings are definitely on that list. So is your spouse/partner if you have or have had one, as well as your children. You will probably be on your own list as well. You don't need to have committed a mortal sin in order to make amends, just put everybody there, get it off your chest. Be thorough, don't start hiding under your chair because you think I am going to ask you to something embarrassing next. Just write the list of everyone you have hurt and do it with humility, honesty, and bravery.

Once you have that list, you'll see that some of the things you have done have a different weight to them. Some harms feel heavier, others are simple and less attached to emotions. Notice that too. You can rank each person in order of the gravity of your actions. Where, for example, telling a white lie to your boss to get out of the holiday party might be a one, cheating on your spouse is a three. This will give you a more accurate view. Chances are you have a lot more ones than threes. But even if you have a lot of threes, there is nothing to be ashamed about. You are working on being better, those actions were taken by your previous iteration of you.

Now, there are two different forms of amends: direct and indirect. Direct is easy, just pick up the phone and have a truthful conversation owning your side of things or pay back the $100 you owe your friend. You can take direct action to amend that. Indirect amends, as you might guess, are more complicated. Maybe the person on your list has died, or you've lost track of them. Or sometimes reaching out to them might cause *them* more harm than good. Let's say you were unfaithful in a relationship and really hurt someone. They are now happily married to someone else. Going back and asking for forgiveness from that person, might make *you* feel better, but it might make them feel bad all over again. In that case, you would make an indirect amend because going back would hurt them more.

Another example: Let's say that way back when in college you cheated on your finals. You cannot ask your college for forgiveness, and you don't even remember your professor's name, but you still remember you cheated; therefore, you would make indirect amends. Here are some examples of direct and indirect amends.

Direct amends:

CALL, SEND an email, letter, Facebook message, send someone a card, pay back debts, or make a payment plan to pay them off, take someone out to coffee or lunch and have a conversation. For children, apologize for losing your patience and if it is not appropriate to talk to them about the subject, spend some time with them doing something that they want to do, make it about them, not about you. Every time you do the right thing, it's a weight off your shoulders; you'll quickly notice a new sense of freedom.

Indirect amends:

TAKE AN action that will benefit someone else, but on behalf of the person you need to make amends to. For example, you need to make amends to Grandma Sue who passed away. You know she loved cats, therefore you donate to the ASPCA in her honor or volunteer to take care of your friend's cat while she is away. The amount doesn't matter, doing it does. In that college example, maybe you could tutor a kid for free for a couple of hours as a way of you paying back the college for having cheated. Or if you were rather mean to an old romantic partner, do something extra nice for your current one in honor of that old relationship. As long as you take the action with intention, and connect it to what you need to amend, you will feel the benefit. That is how you wipe your slate clean. Be creative! Sometimes it's not going to be fun because you have to swallow your pride and have a difficult conversation; but other times you might actually enjoy both the process and the results.

Therefore, once you make your list, write next to them if they are direct or indirect amends, jot down ideas of what you need to do, and then start taking action. Maybe you do one a day, or one a week. Perhaps you come up empty handed with ideas on indirect amends. You don't have to figure it all out right now, but you do need to start. It feels good when you finish cleaning up the relationship with someone, and that good feeling will motivate you to do it again until you get through your list.

All that matters is that you are moving forward. Just that alone will help.

Amazing things happen when you start making amends, relationships you thought were beyond repair may re-flourish. It's pretty magical. Here is my favorite story about making amends.

As YOU know, I grew up in Brazil, and lived there until I was fifteen when I moved to Morocco with my family. In

Brazil, there was a woman who lived in my home since I was two until the day I left. She got married, had a son, and we all lived together. She was my second mom and a huge figure in my life for the more than thirteen years she raised me. Thirteen years is a long time to not have anything to make amends for, so there were a few things for which I felt I needed to ask for forgiveness. But there was no way for me to reach out to her. We had lost touch, it was before social media, and I had no idea where she was or what she was doing. The only thing I had was an old address that may or may not have been where she lived. I wrote her a long, heartfelt, honest letter. I put it in the mail, even if I didn't know if it would ever get to her. I didn't put a return address on the envelope so it could not be returned; I wouldn't know if she ever got it or not. As soon as the letter was in the mail, my amend was made and it would be the end of my guilt over the wrongs I had committed. However, I did write my contact information inside the letter, just in case.

As it turns out, it wasn't her address, but the person who lived there somehow knew her and passed my letter on. Much to my surprise, she reached back out to me. Since then, this woman who is my second mom has been a huge part of my life again. And after all those years of feeling guilty about the things I did, I was not only able to let the guilt go, but also to bring someone who means so much to me back into my life. Miracles happen, but you have to do the work.

The byproduct of my going through this exercise diligently was that integrity became one of my most important values. I *do not* want to go through this exercise again, so I try not to do things that I will need to make amends for. Obviously, I make mistakes, or hurt people without meaning to. I try to make it up to them right then and there. It is simple and easy, and I don't carry big regrets.

In fact, integrity became such a big value of mine we spend a whole week teaching it to children in the EmpowerFit curriculum. When you act with integrity, mistakes are easily forgiven. There was no malice. Even if others are less forgiving, you can have compassion for yourself. If you don't act with integrity, you often hide your mistakes because you were trying to cut corners and it didn't work. Making amends and having integrity go hand in hand, and as far as the power of actions go, this is high up there on the life-changing scale.

NOW THAT you have given yourself permission to work on your 20% of discomfort, and you have cleared (or at least started to clear) the baggage of the past, what action do you take next? Only you will know, but decide to take action, and then, as Nike says, just do it. Take a little step or a giant step, it doesn't matter, but do it. You won't be an entirely new empowered being in one minute, but progress is what we are looking for here.

Can you be just 1% better today than you were yesterday? That's all I am asking for. And if you can, in less than four months you will be 100% better than you are today. You will still have discomfort, yet because you are now looking at that discomfort with appreciation instead of fear, you will realize just how much your life container has grown. You will coexist with discomfort and face it with peace.

One way to know if you are committed to taking actions

to work on your 20% of discomfort is that these actions show up on your calendar and in your pocketbook. If your 20% of discomfort is in health, for example, then a committed decision could be that on your calendar there is time set aside for exercise and you are spending money on a gym membership, trainer, classes, or buying better quality foods. If your 20% discomfort right now is that you are lonely and want a relationship, then your calendar should reflect time for some social activities where you are meeting people, and your bank account will reflect those expenses or even a personal development coach so that you can be the best version of yourself. If you want to know if you are moving forward in addressing your discomfort, check your time and bank account and they will show you just how committed you are to changing.

Amy's Story

THE DAY after Amy invested in starting her business, she called me to say she had made a mistake. She was in the process of getting a divorce and her soon to be ex-husband was not supportive of her new endeavor. Instead of believing in herself, she was believing him. She was stuck in a negative narrative where fear was winning. Big time.

Amy knew why she wanted to start a children's fitness business: she wanted financial freedom, to spend time with her children whom she homeschooled, and to have an impact on her community. What Amy lacked was permission… from herself. This was the first big decision she made solo, and she was afraid of getting it wrong. But the mold she had for her family was broken because of the divorce, things were not going to be how she had dreamed of. But she still hadn't created a new mold for herself. So right then and there, on that phone call, instead of allowing her to back out of the plan she believed would help her most, we spoke about permission. What would happen if she didn't go through with it? How would that fuel the resentment she felt towards her ex-husband? What example was she giving her children? When Amy realized all she needed to do was to give herself permission to follow her own path specially since she was now on her own...it was simple. She stayed on board, started her business, and has worked with hundreds of children in her community.

7.

THE POWER OF RESULTS

2 + 2 MUST EQUAL FOUR

YOUR FIFTH superpower is actually the consequence of how you engage with all of your superpowers. Everything you see is a result of your sequence - your thoughts, words, beliefs, and actions. Where you live, what you do, who is around you... All of those are results of decisions that were made in the past.

....

*Your inputs equal your outputs. You cannot plant
a pumpkin seed and expect to get a pear tree.*

....

BEING CONSCIOUS of your superpowers will influence those results and empower you to change something that is not yet at the level that it could, or you want it to, be.

....

Your results then, depend on you.

....

THIS IS not to point the finger, or to make a blame and shame statement. See it as empowering. If you accept that your results depend on you, then it is much easier to do the work. Using the tools I shared with you in this book will absolutely help you change any result in any area of your life. Results are nothing more than data informing you of where you are today in comparison with yesterday. You can look at your results as feedback. The relationship fell apart and that wasn't the result you were looking for. Okay, I know it hurts, but what is that hurt telling you? What is that failed relationship trying to show you?

Go back to your Life Inventory. Which area did you decide you both wanted to change and were willing to do the work to change? Now, let's examine how you are using your superpowers in that area. For example, let's go back to the health example.

WHAT THOUGHTS do you have regarding your heath? What words do use when it comes to your health?

"I'm fat, I need to diet, I won't stick to it, and I don't exercise enough."

Or,

"I'm getting healthier, I am committed to a good diet, I am making better choices, and I am setting time aside to move my body."

WHAT BELIEFS then, do you have about health?

"Being healthy is hard, time consuming and expensive." Or,
"Being healthy is a habit that I am able to create when I set my mind to it."

WHAT ACTIONS do you take based on those beliefs?

Do you give up at the first cupcake sighting? Or,
Do you go to an exercise class even if you did eat that cupcake?

YOUR RESULTS will reflect how you use your superpowers and reinforce your patterns. Again, taking the health example, you think you are overweight and unhealthy but it's hard to change because you have always been overweight. You take the actions aligned with this belief; therefore, you don't become healthier. Your lack of results will then reinforce the belief that is hard to be healthy and on and on and on.

Here's another example to drive the point home, let's say you chose the area of career.

WHAT THOUGHTS do you have about your career? What

words do you use?

> "I hate my job, I'm stuck, it sucks and I suck at it."
> Or,
> "My job is not what I want it to be, but I have learned skills and I can use those in another position."

WHAT BELIEFS then, do you have about your career?

> "My career is fixed, it has a certain path and I must follow it."
> Or,
> "Though most people follow a certain path in this career, I can find a way to use my skills and do something I enjoy more."

WHAT ACTIONS do you take based on those beliefs?

> Do you tolerate your fate, and spend the rest of your days complaining to your coworkers by the water cooler?
> Or,
> Do you research other fields that might need someone with your skills?

YOUR RESULTS will be dictated by these. You will either stay at the career you tolerate, or you will find another opportunity that better suits you.

I KNOW this sounds redundant, but I want to be 100% clear. Sure, there are circumstances outside of your control that will influence how you use your five superpowers. However, these are *your* powers to use or ignore as you see fit. Change starts with you.

Understanding them and having tools to work with your superpowers is important so you can change what lies underneath and change your results. But the motivation to engage them comes from your discomfort.

And what happens when you tackle your 20% discomfort? You grow as a person. Maybe you are successful in becoming a healthier version of you losing the weight you wanted. Or perhaps you haven't met your goals in the timeline you had set for yourself and realize you have more work to do. Either way results, both positive and negative, inform you and your journey. In truth, the result is not the "outside thing." The result is not really the weight loss, career, or money. The result is the person you become in the process of tackling your discomfort. It's the growth of your life container, it's confidence.

RESULTS BREED CONFIDENCE

CONFIDENCE DOESN'T come from doing something easy; it comes from tackling your 20% of discomfort and overcoming whatever challenge you chose to undertake.

MY BOYS were little the first time I ever went camping. I was apprehensive and only agreed to go despite my reservations because we were going with a family who might as well have been incarnations of Robinson Crusoe. We took a boat to an island off the coast of Miami and pitched a tent for three nights. Everything about this experience was outside my comfort zone. Not only did we purchase our first tent, but I also didn't have a clue of where or how to set it up. That was just the beginning of the laundry list of things I didn't know about sleeping outdoors. From the wind which almost blew us away, to air mattresses that leaked, to children who stepped barefoot on embers, everything was reason to panic simply because I didn't know better. I relied on our camping friends to show me how to do things and know that we were safe. However, when we got off the boat back to Miami, I was standing a little taller. I survived, learned new skills, and felt like I could handle anything just because I spent three nights in a tent.

With my freshly minted confidence in the outdoors, we began to venture out more. Eventually, I agreed to camp just the four of us, no outdoorsy friends to help me feel safe. Our camping experiences became longer expeditions and we have camped all across the country from Yellowstone National Park where elk greeted us in the morning to North Carolina where a thunderstorm literally shook the ground. We eventually bought a camper and even camped in the deep winter in Colorado with freezing temperatures. Our nights in the outdoors are some of my favorite family memories, and those memories which I treasure are the result of tackling my 20% of discomfort in camping.

Confidence is a result of your actions in tackling your 20% of discomfort.

THAT IS why I am passionate about teaching you to embrace discomfort, so you can gain confidence as you grow. Yet, when it comes to our children, we often sabotage a child's opportunity for growth because we worry about hurting their self-esteem.

I'll be the first to raise my hand for being guilty of this. When my boys were born, I was going to be the Perfect Mom and they were going to be the Perfect Children. I read every book known to womankind looking for someone to tell me what to do so that my kids would be okay. Everyone was an expert, and I knew nothing. I was terrified that I was going to hurt my kids or worse, mess them up so badly that they too would end in the psych ward. After all, if addiction is biological and hereditary, my sons are screwed. I was devoted to my boys; as babies they couldn't say so much as "ack" before I was there taking care of their every need.

Therefore, years later, when I began teaching preschool and then coaching a kids' running club, I could absolutely empathize with the mom who doesn't want her child to be damaged, who would bubble wrap her child if she could. I even did a segment on Huff Post Live about being a helicopter mom. I was her...until I learned better.

We've all heard about helicopter parents - those parents who hover over their child not allowing them any space to make their own decisions. In extreme cases, these are the moms who go to their child's job interviews. If I hadn't learned better, that would've likely been me.

But you don't have to be that extreme. You could just want your child to win all the time. Since your child participated in a soccer tournament, surely he should get a medal...even if his team came in eighth place...out of eight...right?

As part of EmpowerFit, the curriculum we teach children, the last week of classes is the medal challenge. Here we push kids to go a bit past their comfort zone and it is always an ordeal...For the parents. I have to send an email the night before the last class to parents to remind them we do not give medals unless the child succeeded in completing the challenge. I assured them we would never ask their child to do something they weren't capable of. I also wrote them that if for whatever reason they did not succeed the first time, we would give them a second, third or tenth chance. It didn't matter how long it took, but they had to complete it in order to earn a medal.

I don't think I could be any clearer and there was always *that* mom. The one who was terrified her child would be the only child in the class who didn't complete the challenge and earn their medal and that this would scar them for life. One of these moms, after receiving my email approached me with a smile from ear to ear. She asked me how many kids were in the class she was going to get a little trophy and goodie bag for each child to take home since it was the end of the season.

Again, I understand. When my sons were little, they "played soccer." I put quotes because at five years old that really isn't playing. My kid sat in the middle of the field and picked his nose for the entire 10 minutes the game would last. He literally did nothing. And at the end? He was beaming with pride when he got a trophy bigger than he was. He showed it to his dad, his grandparents, his teacher, his classmates in show-and-tell, the cashier at the supermarket, the toll booth attendant. Anyone really.

Something in me clicked because here was my son who was beaming that he won a trophy for soccer when he literally did nothing.

As much of a doting mom I am, that was a bit much even for me. The next time he threw a tantrum about something, as young children often do, I thought to myself: *I'm raising an entitled, spoiled little brat.* That was when I learned medals are earned not given. And I made that a central theme in EmpowerFit.

As for the running club mom, I can understand where she was coming from. Her daughter was not the fastest and she was afraid she wouldn't succeed. In order to make it okay for her daughter she would buy trophies for everyone. Of course, every child would love it (she was right about that part). But what she didn't understand is that confidence is the result of overcoming discomfort. By buying a trophy for every child regardless of whether they earned it, she was subconsciously telling her daughter, "I don't believe in you enough that you can do this, so I am going to go through great lengths and make sure you feel okay."

I couldn't control what this mom would do or say to her daughter. But she was not going to manipulate our entire class to make sure her daughter's feelings were not hurt. Can you guess what happened next? Her daughter completed the challenge and earned her medal. The result was confidence not a damaged self-esteem. We think it's love, but it's actually demeaning.

It's easy to see how this applies to children. But it's the same for adults. How many times did you not "put yourself out there" for fear of rejection? Whether that is asking for a promotion or asking someone out on a date. Or what are you tolerating in your life right now because you are afraid of change? Leaving your comfort zone does not guarantee a positive result; but it guarantees confidence. You will either learn that rejection is not such a big deal, or you will create the changes you desire in your life.

DON'T CONFUSE RESULTS WITH GOALS

SOMETIMES WE confuse results with goals. Goals can be large and ambitious and take forever to achieve. They are also moving targets as we talked about before: the whole "I'll be happy when…" phenomenon. If the goalposts keep moving, or we never get to a destination, we feel like we haven't had any success. We feel as if we are always struggling which is very unmotivating as it seems we are working our butts off for nothing.

Therefore, it is important to reframe, and to recognize we have results every step of the way as we move towards our goals. We should celebrate each and every one of them, even if that feels weird or uncomfortable. Having one small success after another builds resilience. The continued reinforcement provides you enough evidence that things are going well, motivating you to continue pursuing your goals. In life, just as in sports, there is momentum. Let's take basketball for example. If the winning team keeps scoring one basket after the other, what does the losing team's coach do? He calls for a timeout. Why? To stop the momentum of the winning team.

....

Winning helps you keep winning.

....

AND YET, when it comes to our lives we tend to focus on the negative momentum, even though it might not be negative at all. Let's say that your 20% of discomfort is that you've always wanted to write a book, but you haven't yet. I'm not talking from personal experience or anything (wink wink). There is an enormous gap from a blank Word document to a printed book. From what the book will be about to what the cover will look like, there is so much that goes into getting these pages to you. But if you make the only result of this process a printed book in your hand, it's going to be a rough road. There is a long lead time where you might lose steam, feel like you can't do it, and maybe even give it up all together. If, however, you define your goal as the printed book, but if every task completed is its own result on the way to that goal, then you will be winning the whole journey. You will build momentum and the process of reaching your goal will be smoother. Break down goals and measure smaller results so that you can be successful every day.

"Wait Cristina, doesn't this go against the whole 'you will always have 20% of discontent' premise?"

NOT REALLY. Your overarching discomfort in this case, is that you have always wanted to be a published author, but you still haven't done it. You tackle that one action at a time, and each of these actions will have its own result. When you string a bunch of those results together you will get to your goal of being a published author.

And then? Then the goal post will move. Maybe you will want to have two books published to feel like a "real" author. Or maybe your discomfort will be that you are not a bestselling author, yet. I don't know what it is, but I'm sure it will be there and that's a positive thing. It doesn't mean I don't stop to acknowledge that not only I tackled that part of my 20%, but I also made my container bigger.

When I signed up for my first Ironman triathlon in Florida, I couldn't believe I had the guts to do that and was freaking out. I trained like a madwoman. When I completed the race, I thought, *Well, sure I did an Ironman, but it was in Florida and there were no mountains.* To be a real Ironman I needed to prove that I could do the distance with the climbs. After my third Ironman I thought, *Sure, I've done three Ironman races, but I've never done a triathlon pulling someone.* The challenges I set for myself were getting larger and larger and my body was breaking down. So much so, I had a full hip replacement before I even turned fifty! What I learned was that each race was just the end of a chapter, not the book. Each chapter had its beginning, middle, and end. The next chapter of growth doesn't have to be a longer distance, it's about who I become. Recognizing this allowed me to celebrate each step and ultimately feel more successful. And the more successful I felt, the easier it was to continue on to the next thing in my 20% of discomfort.

The tool of celebrating small wins is an easy one to use, but oftentimes we make it more complicated than it needs to be. We believe celebrations have to be elaborate or expensive, and that's just not true. I didn't throw a party every time I wrote a paragraph. But when I finished a chapter, I might take the dogs on a walk, consciously breathe in the air, and focus on the gratitude for having something to say. I didn't do this because I am rigid and a nerd; I do it because it always feels good to me. And when I felt good, that reinforced my belief and added more momentum to what I was doing. A celebration can be as simple as a coffee break, a little dance, or a scroll through social media. It's the act of acknowledging the success that matters more.

....

We need to recognize progress in order to continuously create progress.

....

THE SAME applies to all of us who are fond of "to-do lists." For some, these lists are demotivating because they focus on what still needs to be done. Well yeah, there will always be more to do. To others, like me, to-do lists are great motivators because I get to check off and be successful with each action I take. The result I look for is not "I'll happy when all the tasks on my to-do list are crossed off." If that were the case, there is a good chance I'd never be successful. The result of your action is to cross off one task. That is the celebration, that creates momentum. One task, not one list.

But if you are an overachiever like yours truly, one task doesn't seem like a big enough result to pat myself on the back. Fine, then set a goal that you will achieve two results from your list that day and celebrate that. The point is, find a way to win. Winners keep winning. You get to define your goals and make them as huge as you'd like. But noticing your results along the way will build resilience and keep you motivated to continue challenging your 20% of discomfort.

8.

THE NEW BEGINNING

WE WERE in a coffee shop in the middle of nowhere, waiting for the guide who would take us rock climbing at Taos Ski Valley. The coffee shop was picture perfect: adobe, vigas, on a dirt road, in a tiny town. It was so different than our usual bumper to bumper Miami traffic that I turned to Joe and said, "Why not here?"

It was 2017. Both my parents had passed away, and I had been there for fifteen years which in my world might as well be eternity. New Mexico had always called my attention. I had driven through it once going from California to Texas and discovered that it's called the Land of Enchantment for a reason. I was enchanted.

Joe looked at me and said, "Sure, why not?"

One year later, almost to the day, everything we owned was either donated, in storage, or in the two cars we were driving to our new home in Taos, New Mexico.

We came for a year, to test the waters and make sure

that's what we wanted. But in my heart of hearts, I knew we weren't going back. So, when we officially decided to stay in Taos, I told the boys "I am *not* moving from this house until I die." To which Diego sassily replied, "That's what you said last time."

But I meant it. I *loved* that house. It was in a small rural town, and big enough to fit all our friends. We worked on it for years converting the garage to a music room for the boys, adding a woodstove to stay warm on snowy nights, and that garden. I spent hundreds of hours in that garden, mostly killing anything I planted, but it was my Happy Place.

After Joe died, I moved to Santa Fe to be closer to the boys who studied there. Every weekend I'd return to that house, and the heartache returned with me. Country houses don't do well when vacant. My garden was overgrown with weeds, mice had found their way into the music room, and there was a dead bird inside the wooden stove. It was disheartening; I knew I needed to sell it.

Six months after losing Joe, now I was losing my house too. I also lost all my furniture which was too big for our small Santa Fe home. I tried to sell what I could and donated the rest. A very nice couple bought my dresser for $120. As they took it down and into their car, a deep sadness overcame me. I hid so the boys couldn't see me and cried. I had that dresser since the day we got married. It had stored my thin and fat clothes, my maternity clothes, and my triathlon bike shorts. That dresser, and all the memories and stories it stored, was being carried away by two strangers. So was the coffee table I took from my mom's house, and even the chairs that were once at my grandparents' apartment. I felt like my family was crumbling; but that was my pity pot thinking.

Truth is, we could've stayed. I could've made other choices. I could've rented a storage unit. There was a way. There is *always a way*. Yet, the decisions I thought were best for us did not include those choices. I wasn't losing, I was letting go.

Owning that was an important milestone. It was *empowering*. My things were being taken away by strangers, but those people who bought the dresser weren't ripping it from my soul, they purchased it so they could store their own memories in it. I sold it to them, and I managed to find *gratitude*.

I couldn't change the fact that Joe died. He decided to be taken off the ventilator, that was his life and his decision. I was there to support him and advocate for his wishes to be honored and I did. As much as I accept the facts, dying that day was his decision, not mine. At first it felt like an argument that I lost. Over time I began to change my thoughts. The day I left our house, I went room by room and thanked them. Thank you, garage, for hosting so many jam sessions. Thank you, bedroom, where I could hear the cats hunting mice in the spring. Thank you, Joe's office, where he sat and read the news every morning with his cup of coffee. I began to create a belief that Joe is still with me, in our boys, in my memories. He is still a part of me, just not here repeating bad dad jokes on a daily basis. This belief has allowed me to take actions, to move forward, to purchase things and release others. And the results? There are many. Some good, some bad, and some others indifferent. But all of them provide data and context for our new circumstances.

There is a saying in AA that "God doesn't give you more than you can handle." I hated that. Not because of the whole God thing, I'm pretty agnostic to it. But what I would hear is, "Don't get better, because then God will give you more shit to handle." I didn't want more things I needed to "handle," getting sober was hard enough. Maybe you are feeling that way too, at the end of this journey we've had together. If it's this hard to handle our current 20% of discomfort, and it never goes away, it just gets bigger as our life gets bigger ... why go through the trouble?

If you were one of my students, I'd ask you to come closer and lean in now. To my PreK class, that was a sign that Ms. Cristina was going to say something special. You can handle the 20% of discomfort that you have today. You cannot handle the 20% discomfort you will have in ten years when hopefully your life is bigger and better. The good news is you don't have to. You are not that person yet. All you have to do is believe that the "ten years in the future you" will have learned a whole lot going through your current discomfort and will have the skills to tackle your discontent then. Even though life is bigger, your larger 20% of discomfort won't feel more overwhelming because you have grown too. Right now, all you have is right now.

My life today is infinitely bigger than my life when I got sober and met Joe. Children, animals, houses, schools, family vacations, accidents, friends ... all these things have come to me between then and now. The discomfort I had my first year as a widow was gut wrenching, but it was 20% of this bigger life. It sucked, don't get me wrong; but I rose to the occasion as anyone could. Twenty years ago, I was in a psych ward because a boyfriend dumped me, I could barely handle that. Today, I am writing this book after my husband died. I couldn't fathom this situation twenty years ago. But even now, even if I knew Joe would die at fifty-seven after twenty years together, I would still have married him all over again. I would never risk not having had the life I have now.

If you would've told me four years ago when I started expanding my business that close to two hundred women were going to start their independent businesses to teach my EmpowerFit curriculum to over ten thousand children … I don't think I would've believed you. The Cristina of 2018 couldn't handle that vision and would focus only on the problems that would bring. But the Cristina of 2023 sure can. And if I'm lucky, in another twenty years my life (along with my 20% of discomfort) will continue growing; and I will be able to handle it then as I do now, as I did when I got sober.

Sometimes life sucks. There are just no two ways about it. More often than not, life is beautiful. I hope this book has given you a new perspective on discomfort. You may not have my flavor of discontent, but you bear your own burdens. I honor that in you. I see you and I feel you. And because I do, I challenge you to go in there. Do something about it, face your fears, and overcome your obstacles. On the other side of it will be growth, a new empowered you feeling like a total badass for having conquered your 20% of discomfort. And though being unphased about future challenges might be a stretch, know that when your container grows, you will grow *with it* and will be able to handle whatever life throws your way.

But what can you do right now? First is become aware and start honing your superpowers. Pay attention to your thoughts, words, and beliefs. See the connections between them and your actions and results. Awareness is empowerment because even if you don't do one darn thing about it, it will be your choice. You aren't just a victim of your circumstance, now you know exactly what you need to do to face it. Sometimes that is not so easy, and if you are stuck then seek help. There is always help just as there is always a solution. Speak to someone, join one of our coaching programs, get a friend and go through the exercises in this book together, take some more personal development courses, there are many ways to turn these pages into your life changing results.

....

As you grow, the world will grow with you.

....

LIFE WILL present you with more opportunities as well as more obstacles. Now you know that is part of the deal. So what? Sometimes that is scary. Feel the fear, do it anyways.

You will not be a completely different person when you wake up tomorrow just because you read this book. But it doesn't have to take forever either. Every time you exercise one of your superpowers, there is a ripple effect out there in the world.

Let's continue with our previous health example. Let's say you tackled your discomfort and one of your actions was to run a 5k race (sounds familiar?). Because of that new action, your children will have better health habits from seeing you train, your co-workers might be inspired and start their own journey, you may join a team and meet wonderful people and create lifelong friendships, you might run for a cause and raise funds for a nonprofit, and with your donation that nonprofit might be able to now offer life changing services to someone else. Who knows?

I don't know the details, but I know you. I believe that you can do whatever it is you want to. And as one of my coaches was fond of saying, I am getting my popcorn out to watch you as you grow.

Let's GO. It's power time.

Did you learn something new in this book? I'd be so grateful if you could leave a quick review. It takes less than sixty seconds and goes a long way in helping others be empowered too.

Thank you for spreading the word!

www.CristinaMRamirez.com/amazonreviews

Or, scan here with your phone!

ABOUT THE AUTHOR

Cristina Ramirez is a serial entrepreneur and empowerment coach helping clients redefine what is possible for themselves, their families, and their communities.

Cristina created the EmpowerFit™ Curriculum for teaching growth mindset through running. Her empowerment lessons have been taught to over ten thousand children through the DashStrøm Run Club network where she empowers mothers to start their independent children's fitness business. The curriculum is also available through the EmpowerFit™ Certification Program.

In addition, EmpowerFit™ has been adapted for corporations and institutions bringing an innovative approach to workforce development programs.

When not feverishly empowering someone, you will find her snowboarding with her sons, hiking with her dogs, or cleaning the cat litter.

For more information or to book trainings and speaking engagements, please visit: www.cristinaMramirez.com

ACKNOWLEDGMENTS

I'VE ALWAYS wanted to write a book, I just didn't know how. If it weren't for the guidance and support of so many, *Empowered by Discomfort* wouldn't have come into existence. I cannot express my gratitude enough. This is my life's work and I have never been so meticulous about anything before!

It took a village to give me the courage to put myself out there, and then to get through to the other side. First, a very special thank you to James Reich, for patiently editing, designing, and putting up with my intensity. Also to Angelita Canoy Capadocia, who always finds a way to figure things out and keeps our process moving forward. Finally, a huge thanks to my friends and family for allowing me the space to write, cry, doubt, grieve, and eventually triumph. I love you all.

And of course, to all the Kickstarter Backers who pledged their support very early on, at all levels of the campaign. I was blown away by your enthusiasm and generosity. And a special thank you to the following Kickstarter backers:

Aimee Turner
Amanda Morell
Amy Melnicsak
Anne Rothe
Audrey Pinney
Bia de Molina
Carina Ramirez Cahan
Carmen Medrano
Caryn Lubetsky
Christina Windeler
Christine Rivas Glauerdt
Claire Ketchum
Cristina Macias Amador
Dayna English
Donna de Molina
E Poon
Elena de Molina
Gail Bray
Gayle R. De Los Santos
Gustavo Lipsztein
Helen O'Shaughnessy
Jill Vickers
Julie Thomas
Julie A Knoblauch
Lisa Edmonds
Lourdes Forcade Farinas
Mahi Livain
Maite Albanese

Manuela
Maria and Eric Duehring
Maria Lucia Bradfield Garcia
Melissa Cancio
Monica Blower
Tonya Pacanins
Myriam Fizazi-Hawkins
Nancy Heydinger
Nena Woolworth
Olayinka Ewuola
Paolo Pellecer
Rita Ramirez
Ryan Beckwith
Samantha and Charlie Wykoff
Sean Cotton
Sondra
Stacey Ramirez
Steve Burns
Susan DeLand
Anna Tereza Alcantara Machado
Vivian Calienes
Yuris Fuentes

✺